THE Instant Kitchen MEAL PREP Cookbook

THE Instant Kitchen MEAL PREP Cookbook

Plan and Cook Ahead for Fast,
Family-Friendly Meals
Using Your Pressure Cooker and Air Fryer

Coco Morante

Photography by Dana Gallagher

HARVEST
An Imprint of WILLIAM MORROW

 For information, address HarperCollins Publishers, 195 Broadway, New York, NY 10007. In Europe, HarperCollins Publishers, Macken House, 39/40 Mayor Street Upper, Dublin 1, D01 C9W8, Ireland.

HarperCollins books may be purchased for educational, business, or sales promotional use. For information, please email the Special Markets Department at SPsales@harpercollins.com.

hc.com

FIRST EDITION

Designed by Tai Blanche

Photography by Dana Gallagher

Food Styling: Cyd Raftus McDowell

Food Styling Assistants: Tommy McKiernan and Debbie Kim

Recipe icons by Tai Blanche

Shopping list background pattern © ELENA/stock.adobe.com

Library of Congress Cataloging-in-Publication Data

Names: Morante, Coco author | Gallagher, Dana other
Title: The instant kitchen meal prep cookbook : plan and cook ahead for fast, family-friendly meals using your pressure cooker and air fryer / Coco Morante ; photography by Dana Gallagher.
Description: First edition. | New York, NY : Harvest, an imprint of William Morrow, [2025] | Includes index. |
Identifiers: LCCN 2025008674 (print) | LCCN 2025008675 (ebook) | ISBN 9780063360068 paperback | ISBN 9780063360075 ebook
Subjects: LCSH: Quick and easy cooking | One-dish meals | Smart cookers | Hot air frying | LCGFT: Cookbooks
Classification: LCC TX833.5 .M668 2025 (print) | LCC TX833.5 (ebook) | DDC 641.5/12—dc23/eng/20250319
LC record available at https://lccn.loc.gov/2025008674
LC ebook record available at https://lccn.loc.gov/2025008675

ISBN 978-0-06-336006-8

25 26 27 28 29 PCA 10 9 8 7 6 5 4 3 2 1

To all the hardworking parents
getting dinner on the table,
this one's for you.

CONTENTS

Simply Organic
minced onion
Just
Sweet paprika

INTRODUCTION

I'm sure a lot of people have a situation like mine: children to feed, a busy schedule, and a need for fast, budget-conscious recipes. Friends, this book is for you.

Thankfully, we already have a lot of great tools to help us streamline our grocery shopping and cooking routines. There's curbside pickup for the groceries and kitchen technologies like pressure cooking and air frying to keep things simple and fast . . .

And then there's the planning and prepping. I don't know how many times I have thought, during yet another busy week, I wish somebody would just tell me what to do in the kitchen. *Hey Coco, here's what you should prepare ahead and pop in the fridge while you've got a free minute or two. And here's how you're going to pull it all together for stress-free mealtimes.*

As it turns out, nobody has shown up thus far to order me around in my kitchen. That somebody had to be me, I guess, the seasoned cookbook author (who knew, right?), so I went ahead and wrote the book I'd wished for. And this book is as much for me as it is for you, providing us a variety of make-ahead breakfasts and meal-prepped dinners that have become the building blocks for my family's weekday meal plans.

Unlike any other meal prep cookbook out there, this one makes use of my two favorite pieces of kitchen technology: the air fryer and the electric pressure cooker. Cooking with these appliances will speed up and simplify your meal prep and reheating, so feeding your family homecooked meals will become more doable and less time consuming.

You'll take advantage of the rest of your kitchen as well, cooking with an oven, stove, and microwave when they make the most sense. Realistically, most of us are going to be meal prepping in a kitchen that has more appliances than just a pressure cooker and air fryer, after all! I'm not about air frying or pressure cooking something just because you can.

You'll find 10 weeks' worth of meal plans here, providing your family with a wide variety of delicious dinners that appeal to adults and kids alike. Have a baby or small child at the table? No problem! These meals have components that you can feed to babies, too, so you're never stuck heating up something separate for the little ones.

The rest of the book consists of make-ahead breakfasts (along with a selection of last-minute morning ideas), my favorite small-batch baked goods, some simple lunches, and the laziest last-minute dinners to rely on when you're not in planning-ahead mode. I've got you covered for every meal.

Here's to finding kitchen solutions that make our lives a little easier, and giving ourselves lots of grace as we meet challenges along the way. We can do it!

How to Use This Book

This cookbook contains 10 weekly dinner plans. Each one consists of a shopping list, some prep tasks to tackle on Sunday, and simple instructions for putting your evening meals together from Monday through Thursday.

Of course, we all need to feed ourselves more meals than just dinners. In addition to the weekly dinner plans, I've included:

- breakfasts you can make ahead and store in the fridge or freezer, to be reheated on busy mornings, as well as ideas for when you haven't made anything in advance
- lunches that make use of leftovers or pantry staples or involve no cooking at all
- baked goods, savory and sweet—think breads and treats that you can pull together quickly on your own, or involve kids for a fun activity
- last-minute dinners that rely on store-bought prepared foods, for nights when you haven't planned ahead and want to get a wholesome meal on the table, fast

To set yourself up for a successful week of homemade meals, pick a weekly dinner plan on Saturday and get your grocery shopping done using the included shopping list. Then, on Sunday, complete the list of prep tasks, which include chopping up produce, throwing together (mostly no-cook) sauces and vinaigrettes, marinating proteins, and parcooking foods that reheat well. During the week, you'll refer to the "Serve It Up" instructions for each meal, using your pre-prepped ingredients to make dinner a breeze.

A few ground rules to note:

1. I'm assuming you have some basics on hand: salt (more on this below), black pepper, olive oil, and a neutral-flavored oil such as avocado, canola, or vegetable oil. I won't be including those in the shopping lists.
2. Regarding salt, I always use Diamond kosher, but you are welcome to salt your food with whichever kind you prefer. Diamond kosher salt is quite fluffy, so you will need to adjust the quantity down if you are using a denser salt, such as Morton's kosher salt, sea salt, or table salt. And of course, always salt to taste. I start with a moderate amount since I'm serving small children who generally don't need a lot of sodium in their diets.
3. As for other herbs, spices, and seasonings, I also don't include these basics in the shopping lists: garlic powder, onion powder, chili powder, and Italian seasoning.
4. In the shopping lists, you'll find specific quantities of ingredients used in the recipes. For instance, I might call for buying 2 garlic cloves, when most likely you'll need to buy a whole head

of garlic at the store. That way, if you've already got a few cloves of garlic on hand, you will know that you have enough for the week's plan.

With that out of the way, you're ready to dig in. There's no need to go in order. Just find a chapter that looks good to you and get started.

Why Meal Prep with an Air Fryer and Pressure Cooker?

It may seem like I've shoe-horned these appliances into a meal prep book, but they really are lifesavers when it comes to my cooking, meal prep–based and otherwise. Not a day goes by that my husband and I don't rely on our air fryer or pressure cooker to speed up the process of preparing or reheating a meal.

Often, air frying can literally cut in half the time you'll spend heating up your food. Air fryers preheat in about 3 minutes, compared to 10 to 15 minutes for a conventional oven, and they cook the food much faster, too. One example is something I make all the time: roasted vegetables. Start to finish, they take just 15 to 20 minutes in the air fryer, including the preheating time.

As for the pressure cooker, it allows me to be completely hands-off and tend to other kitchen (or life) tasks while the food is cooking. I'm the queen of letting rice, pasta, or beans boil over on the stovetop, but that's virtually impossible with a pressure cooker. You just press a button and walk away.

As far as your kitchen technology goes, in addition to a pressure cooker and air fryer of some sort (basket- or toaster oven–style), I'm also assuming you've got a microwave, a stove, an oven, a food processor, and a blender (pitcher- and/or immersion-style). Some tasks are best suited to one appliance over another, and I'm not going to use one just for the sake of a gimmick or trend.

Making Time for Meal Prep

When I first started approaching each week with meal prep in mind, it seemed very daunting. So much planning and thought had to go into picking the recipes, shopping for them, and figuring out what to get ready in advance and what to leave to the last minute so it wouldn't feel like we were just eating reheated food all week long. All that thinking is what led me to write this cookbook, actually. I wanted a blueprint for myself, to streamline the process and make it less intimidating.

When you put aside a couple hours on a Sunday to prepare for the week, you're investing in your own sanity for the days to come. You'll love how simple it is to take the components you've prepped in advance and quickly get dinner on the table. All the "Serve It Up" instructions are meant to be completed in 30 minutes or less (usually much less), and you'll never find yourself chopping, slicing, or dicing on a weeknight. This means faster dinners, fewer dishes to wash, and a cleaner kitchen throughout the week.

I've divided the meal prep tasks into categories: no cook, pressure cooker, and air fryer. You'll also see icons for stovetop, oven, and microwave when those cooking methods are required.

Of course you can always cook on your stovetop instead of using a pressure cooker, and in a conventional oven instead of an air fryer. I generally dive into the no-cooking-required tasks first, then prep anything that requires heat next. By the time I'm done, everything's stored away, and the kitchen is clean, I feel so excited to get into the week ahead.

Oh, and don't feel like you need to follow a strict meal prep schedule every week if that doesn't work for you! You're not a failure if you don't always plan perfectly. Some weekends are busier than others, and there's no time to shop on Saturday and cook on Sunday. And those are the times I rely on the last-minute ideas in the last section of this book.

Meals for All Ages

One thing you'll find about this book—it's very family friendly. Every meal includes dishes you can enjoy at pretty much any age. This comes from personal experience; in my day-to-day life, I'm making dinner for a toddler, a preschooler, and two middle-aged adults. We all have different likes and dislikes, and of course feeding young kids comes with its own set of challenges and rules.

When it was time to introduce my older daughter to solid foods, I didn't adhere to any prescriptive system. I made some purees, bought some jars and pouches, and gave her "grown-up" food from the table when it made sense. When my second kiddo came along, I found that it was simpler to follow a baby-led feeding strategy most of the time, giving her whatever foods we were eating. This involved a little more forethought in creating adult-friendly meals with baby-friendly options, but ultimately less work, since I wasn't making and buying so many extra foods.

If you're ever unsure about how to safely feed specific foods to a baby or toddler, Solid Starts (SolidStarts.com) is an amazing resource. You can look up just about any food and find information on how to serve it, along with helpful photographs and videos.

Most importantly, if you are dealing with potential food allergies or other feeding challenges, follow the advice of your pediatrician or family doctor.

Meal Prep Pantry Staples

As mentioned previously, this book assumes you've got salt, oil, and a few basic seasonings on hand. Besides those, here are some pantry staples you're going to be seeing over and over in this book:

Baking Basics

It is almost always more economical (and more delicious) to bake things from scratch rather than buying them at the store. It's also a surefire way to get kids involved in the kitchen—they love to measure, pour, and stir. We always have these ingredients in the cupboard:

- All-purpose flour
- Almond flour
- Cornmeal
- Rolled oats
- Baking powder
- Baking soda
- Instant yeast
- Granulated sugar
- Brown sugar (light or dark is fine)
- Cocoa powder
- Chocolate chips
- Sprinkles

And in the fridge, I usually have buttermilk, plain yogurt (Greek or regular), eggs, and butter. With all of that on hand, I'm ready to bake just about anything.

Spices and Spice Blends

In addition to garlic powder, onion powder, chili powder, and Italian seasoning, you'll always find these spices and blends in my cabinet:

- Garlic salt
- Seasoned salt
- Lemon pepper (I'm partial to Lawry's for these first three items.)
- Cayenne pepper
- Red pepper flakes
- Old Bay seasoning
- Cajun or Creole seasoning (I like Tony Chachere's.)
- Pumpkin pie spice
- Za'atar
- Dried oregano
- Dried dill weed
- Paprika (sweet and smoked)
- Ground cumin
- Ground coriander
- Ground turmeric
- Ground cinnamon
- Ground nutmeg

And a few wild cards from Trader Joe's. My family loves their Pizza Sprinkle Seasoning, Seasoning in a Pickle (seasonal), Aglio Olio, Everything but the Bagel, Cuban-Style Citrusy Garlic, and Cheesy Seasoning blends. Whatever your favorite brands or varieties, it's convenient to keep some seasoning blends on hand to liven up your cooking.

Pastas, Grains, and Beans

These are the basis for so many meals. When my shelves are stocked with a few pastas, grains, and beans, I know I can throw something together that my kids will enjoy. As pasta goes, I mostly reach for shorter shapes, with the exception of spaghetti, a forever classic. Rotating between a few different shapes of pasta helps keep things interesting. We also cook a lot of rice—basic long-grain white rice and fragrant jasmine rice are favorites in my house. Some ramen, rice noodles, couscous, quinoa, and oats round out the pantry.

Pastas and grains:

- Spaghetti
- Rotini
- Penne
- Elbows or cavatappi (for mac 'n' cheese)
- Orecchiette
- Orzo
- Pearl couscous
- Ramen noodles (wheat or rice)
- Rice noodles
- Long- and medium-grain white rice
- White jasmine rice
- Quinoa

Beans and other legumes:

- Black beans (or pinto beans if you prefer)
- White beans (such as great northern or navy)
- Chickpeas (aka garbanzo beans)
- Lentils (green or brown)
- Baby lima beans (frozen)
- Edamame (frozen)

Nuts, Seeds, and Dried Fruits

Nuts and dried fruits will take you a long way in jazzing up your meals, and they make great snacks, too. The ones we keep on hand are:

- Raisins, dried cranberries, cherries, and/or blueberries (to add to baked oatmeal and muffins)
- Cashews (the perfect base for dairy-free sauces, and good for snacking, too)
- Walnuts, almonds, and pecans (all available cheap in bulk at Costco, great for snacking or adding to store-bought cereal, granola, or muesli)

Condiments and Sauces

I am not above using store-bought condiments. I rely on them to add flavor and simplify my cooking. Here are some favorites that are always in our pantry or fridge:

- Sriracha and/or sambal oelek (We're Huy Fong loyalists.)
- BBQ sauce (We love Primal Kitchen, Stubb's, Bachan, and HYCH.)
- Marinara sauce (We love Carbone and Rao's.)
- Soy sauce (I get organic Kikkoman from the Japanese grocery store.)
- Mayonnaise (We use Best Foods/Hellmann's or homemade.)
- Mustard (We stock French's yellow, Maille Dijon, and Trader Joe's whole-grain Dijon.)
- Peanut butter (We like Kirkland from Costco; their almond butter is great, too.)
- Tahini (I think Soom is the best brand, at least as far as what's widely available in the US.)

Oils and Vinegars

I tend to keep it simple when it comes to cooking oils—olive oil for Mediterranean-inspired meals and avocado oil for just about everything else, since it's neutral in flavor and has a high smoke point. As for vinegars, it's nice to have a variety, since they each add their own special something to different cuisines. Apple cider vinegar is all I'll use in an American-style coleslaw, and only rice vinegar will do when I make East/Southeast Asian–inspired dressings and sauces or want a milder flavor. Here are my go-tos:

- Olive oil
- Avocado oil (or other neutral-flavored oil)
- Avocado cooking spray (or other neutral-flavored cooking spray)
- Red wine vinegar
- White wine vinegar
- Apple cider vinegar
- Unseasoned rice vinegar
- Balsamic vinegar

Miscellaneous

These items don't fit into one of the above categories exactly, but I always have them on hand and use them often.

- Chicken and/or vegetable broth or broth concentrate (Better Than Bouillon is always in my fridge, and I like Kirkland chicken bone broth for both sipping and cooking.)
- Canned tomatoes and tomato paste
- Panko breadcrumbs
- Honey, maple syrup, or agave nectar
- Dill pickles
- Capers
- Black olives

There are other odds and ends in my pantry, but the above lists are the ones that are always replaced when we run out. It's not necessary (or all that practical) to stock a pantry all at once. Add a couple spices and condiments to your pantry week by week, as you try new recipes and dishes that require new ingredients. And every few months, make sure to go through your pantry to see if anything is nearing its best-by date and needs to be used up—this will help you save money in the long run.

Part 1

HOME RUN MEAL PLANS

Week 1

SAVORY SENSATIONS

Start your week with a Hawaiian-inspired meal of tender kalua-style pork and cabbage, served with my girls' favorite, fluffy steamed rice. Next, enjoy rotisserie-spiced chicken drumsticks, air-fried to crispy skin perfection, with a piquant and punchy salsa verde on the side. On the third night, repurpose leftover pork into saucy sliders, served alongside sweet potato JoJos, aka thick-cut, well-seasoned fries, with honey mustard sauce for dipping. Finally, a Taiwan-inspired meal of tofu and rice noodles in a savory peanut sesame sauce is served alongside crunchy cucumbers marinated in a simple soy dressing.

Week 1 Menu

Kalua-Style Pork and Cabbage, Steamed Rice

Roasted Drumsticks, Zucchini and Carrot Coins, Salsa Verde

BBQ Pulled Pork Sliders, Sweet Potato JoJos, Honey-Mustard Sauce

Peanut-Sesame Tofu and Noodles, Taiwan-Inspired Cucumber Salad

SHOPPING LIST

PRODUCE

- 4 large carrots
- 2 large zucchini (about 1 pound)
- 2 large sweet potatoes (about 1½ pounds)
- 1 (2-pound) green cabbage
- 1 large English cucumber
- 3 garlic cloves
- 1 bunch fresh flat-leaf parsley
- 1 lemon

PANTRY

- 2½ teaspoons garlic salt
- 1½ teaspoons granulated sugar
- 1 teaspoon seasoned salt
- 1 teaspoon paprika
- ⅛ teaspoon cayenne pepper
- ½ cup mayonnaise
- 5½ tablespoons soy sauce
- ¼ cup smooth natural peanut butter
- ¼ cup barbecue sauce
- 3 tablespoons honey
- 3 tablespoons yellow mustard
- ¼ cup unseasoned rice vinegar or fresh lime juice
- 2⅓ tablespoons toasted sesame oil
- 2 tablespoons capers
- 1½ tablespoons agave nectar
- 2 teaspoons sambal oelek or sriracha (optional)
- 1 teaspoon Dijon mustard
- 1½ cups medium-grain white rice
- 1 (14-ounce) package pad thai noodles
- 16 dinner rolls (or use homemade)

PROTEIN

- 8 chicken drumsticks
- 1 (14- to 16-ounce) package firm tofu
- 4 pounds boneless pork shoulder country ribs

DAIRY

- 1 teaspoon butter

SUNDAY MEAL PREP RECIPES

no cook

pressure cooker

air fryer

oven

stovetop

microwave

1.

Seasoned Chicken Drumsticks

Serves 4 to 6

8 chicken drumsticks
1 teaspoon seasoned salt
1 teaspoon garlic salt
¼ teaspoon ground black pepper

Season the drumsticks all over with the seasoned salt, garlic salt, and pepper. Transfer to a zip-top bag or lidded container, label "Seasoned Chicken Drumsticks," and store in the fridge up to 2 days.

2.

Zucchini and Carrot Coin Prep

Serves 4

2 large zucchini (about 1 pound)
4 large carrots

Slice the zucchini and carrots into ¼-inch-thick slices, with either a crinkle cutter or a knife. Transfer to a zip-top bag or lidded container, label "Zucchini and Carrot Coin Prep," and store in the fridge.

Salsa Verde

Makes about ¾ cup

1 cup fresh flat-leaf parsley leaves
2 garlic cloves, peeled
2 tablespoons capers
¼ cup olive oil
1 tablespoon fresh lemon juice
1 teaspoon Dijon mustard
¼ teaspoon kosher salt
⅛ teaspoon ground black pepper

Combine all the ingredients in a wide-mouth pint jar. Lower an immersion blender into the jar and blend at **HIGH** speed for about 45 seconds, until smooth. (Alternatively, blend all the ingredients in a countertop blender, then transfer to a jar.) Label "Salsa Verde" and store in the fridge.

Sweet Potato Wedge Prep

Serves 4

2 large sweet potatoes (about 1½ pounds), scrubbed

Slice the sweet potatoes into 1-inch-thick wedges. Transfer to a zip-top bag or lidded container, label "Sweet Potato Wedge Prep," and store in the fridge.

JoJo Seasoning

Makes 1 batch

1 teaspoon paprika
1 teaspoon garlic salt
½ teaspoon onion powder
¼ teaspoon ground black pepper
⅛ teaspoon cayenne pepper

Add the paprika, garlic salt, onion powder, black pepper, and cayenne pepper to a small jar or other lidded container. Label "JoJo Seasoning" and store at room temperature.

Honey-Mustard Sauce

Makes about ¾ cup

½ cup mayonnaise
3 tablespoons honey
3 tablespoons yellow mustard
¼ teaspoon ground black pepper

Combine all the ingredients in a wide-mouth pint jar and stir until evenly mixed. Label "Honey Mustard Sauce" and store in the fridge.

Peanut-Sesame Sauce

Makes about 2/3 cup

- 1/4 cup smooth natural peanut butter
- 2 tablespoons soy sauce
- 2 tablespoons unseasoned rice vinegar or fresh lime juice
- 1 1/2 tablespoons agave nectar
- 1 tablespoon toasted sesame oil
- 2 teaspoons sambal oelek or sriracha (optional)
- 1/2 teaspoon garlic powder

Combine all the ingredients in a wide-mouth pint jar. Lower an immersion blender into the jar and blend at **HIGH** speed for about 30 seconds, until smooth. (Alternatively, blend all the ingredients in a countertop blender, then transfer to a jar.) It will be quite thick. Taste for sweetness and spice, adding more agave nectar or sriracha, if you like. Label "Peanut-Sesame Sauce" and store in the fridge.

Sesame-Soy Tofu

Serves 4

- 1 (14- to 16-ounce) package firm tofu, drained and cut into 1-inch pieces
- 2 tablespoons soy sauce
- 2 teaspoons toasted sesame oil

Add all the ingredients to a zip-top bag or lidded container. Label "Sesame-Soy Tofu" and store in the fridge.

Cucumber Salad Dressing

Makes about ¼ cup

- 1½ tablespoons soy sauce
- 2 tablespoons unseasoned rice vinegar
- 2 teaspoons toasted sesame oil
- 1½ teaspoons granulated sugar
- 1 garlic clove, minced or pressed

Combine all the ingredients in a half-pint jar or other small lidded container. Shake to combine. Label "Cucumber Salad Dressing" and store in the fridge.

Cabbage Wedge Prep

Serves 4

- 1 medium green cabbage (about 2 pounds)

Cut off a thin layer of any browning at the base of the cabbage, but leave the core intact. Slice the cabbage into 2-inch-thick wedges. Transfer to a zip-top bag or lidded container, label "Cabbage Wedge Prep," and store in the fridge.

Simple Shredded Pork and Pork Broth

Makes 2 batches

4 pounds boneless pork shoulder country ribs, cut in half crosswise

1 tablespoon kosher salt

1 teaspoon garlic powder

2 teaspoons avocado oil or other neutral oil

Season the pork all over with the salt and garlic powder.

Heat the oil in the pressure cooker on the **SAUTÉ** setting for a minute or two. Add half of the pork to the pot in a single layer and let them sear for 5 minutes. Add the rest of the pork to the pot and pour in 1 cup water.

Pressure-cook the pork for 30 minutes at **HIGH** pressure, with a 20-minute **NATURAL** pressure release.

Transfer the pork to a sheet pan, leaving the liquid in the pot, and use two forks to shred the meat into bite-size chunks. Let cool to room temperature, then divide the pork evenly between two lidded containers or zip-top bags. Label one "Pork for Kalua-Style Pork and Cabbage" and the other "Pork for BBQ Pulled Pork Sliders" and store in the fridge.

Pour any cooking liquid from the pot into a quart jar. Label "Pork Broth" and store in the fridge.

Meal 1

Kalua-Style Pork and Cabbage, Steamed Rice

Serves 4

Pork for Kalua-Style Pork and Cabbage (page 18)
Pork Broth (page 18)
1½ cups medium-grain white rice
Cabbage Wedge Prep (page 17)
Avocado oil spray

Add the pork and broth to the pressure cooker. Place a raised wire steam rack in the pot, and place a 1½-quart stainless-steel bowl on the rack. Add the rice and 1½ cups water to the bowl. Pressure-cook the pork and rice for 10 minutes at **LOW** pressure, with a 10-minute **NATURAL** pressure release.

While the pork and rice are cooking, preheat the air fryer to 375°F. Add the cabbage in a single layer directly in the air fryer basket or on the baking sheet of an air fryer oven, lined with parchment paper or aluminum foil. Spray the cabbage wedges all over with avocado oil. Air-fry for 12 minutes.

Transfer the cabbage, rice, and pork to serving plates, spooning some of the broth over the pork and cabbage. Serve right away.

Meal 2

Roasted Drumsticks, Zucchini and Carrot Coins, Salsa Verde

Serves 4

- Seasoned Chicken Drumsticks (page 13)
- Zucchini and Carrot Coin Prep (page 13)
- 1 teaspoon butter
- ½ teaspoon garlic salt
- Salsa Verde (page 14)
- 8 dinner rolls, store-bought or homemade (page 206)

Preheat the air fryer to 375°F. Add the drumsticks in a single layer directly in the air fryer basket or on the baking sheet of an air fryer oven, lined with parchment paper or aluminum foil, and air-fry for 25 minutes.

While the drumsticks are cooking, pour a cup of water into the pressure cooker. Add the zucchini and carrots to a steamer basket and place it in the pot. Pressure-cook for 1 minute at **HIGH** pressure, with a **QUICK** pressure release. Remove the steamer basket from the pot, pour out the water, then return the vegetables to the pot. Add the butter and garlic salt and toss to combine.

Transfer the drumsticks and vegetables to serving plates and serve right away, with the salsa verde and rolls on the side.

Meal 3

BBQ Pulled Pork Sliders, Sweet Potato JoJos, Honey-Mustard Sauce

Serves 4

- Sweet Potato Wedge Prep (page 14)
- JoJo Seasoning (page 15)
- 1 tablespoon avocado oil or other neutral oil
- Simple Shredded Pork (page 18)
- ¼ cup barbecue sauce, plus more for serving
- 8 dinner rolls, store-bought or homemade (page 206)
- Honey-Mustard Sauce (page 15)

Preheat the air fryer to 375°F. In their container or zip-top bag, toss the sweet potato wedges with the JoJo seasoning and oil until evenly coated. Add the sweet potato wedges in a single layer directly in the air fryer basket or on the baking sheet of an air fryer oven, lined with parchment paper or aluminum foil, and air-fry for 15 minutes.

While the potatoes are cooking, heat up the pork: In a microwave-safe bowl, toss the pork with the barbecue sauce. Microwave for 2 minutes. Stir, then microwave for 1 minute more.

Serve the shredded pork on the dinner rolls, with the potatoes and honey-mustard sauce on the side.

NOTE: I like to pair this dinner with some crudités (sliced bell peppers, carrot sticks, and/or celery), which can also be dipped in the honey-mustard sauce.

Meal 4

Peanut-Sesame Tofu and Noodles, Taiwan-Inspired Cucumber Salad

Serves 4

- 1 large English cucumber
- 1 teaspoon kosher salt
- Cucumber Salad Dressing (page 17)
- Sesame-Soy Tofu (page 16)
- 1 (14-ounce) package pad thai noodles
- Peanut-Sesame Sauce (page 16)

Bring 3 quarts of water to a boil in a big pot.

Slice the cucumber into ¼-inch-thick rounds and add to a bowl. Sprinkle the salt over the cucumber and toss to evenly distribute the salt. Let sit for 15 minutes, drain off any excess liquid, then add the cucumber salad dressing and toss to combine.

While the cucumbers are sitting, preheat the air fryer to 350°F. Add the tofu in a single layer directly in the air fryer basket or on the baking sheet of an air fryer oven, lined with parchment paper or aluminum foil, and air-fry for 15 minutes.

When the water comes to a boil, remove it from the heat and add the noodles. Let the noodles soak in the water for 6 minutes, or until they're pliable and al dente. Drain the noodles in a colander, rinse them with cold water, then transfer to a bowl and toss with the peanut-sesame sauce.

Transfer the noodles, tofu, and cucumbers to serving plates. Serve right away.

Week 2

FRESH AND ZESTY

Enjoy an English-inspired dish of lemon pepper cod and peas, followed by burrito bowl night, a favorite in my house. Next up is pasta with a pesto that includes my kids' favorite vegetable, broccoli, alongside flavorful chicken cutlets. Finally, a Mediterranean-meets-Middle-Eastern meal of kabobs, pitas, zucchini, and a tangy, creamy yogurt sauce. A wide variety of flavors will have you looking forward to every dinner!

Week 2 Menu

Lemon Pepper Cod, Tartar Sauce, Minty Peas, Carrot and Potato Mash

Ground Beef Burrito Bowls

Broccoli Pesto Penne with Italian Herb–Marinated Chicken Cutlets

No-Skewer Kabobs, Za'atar Pitas, Herbed Zucchini Coins, Cucumber-Yogurt Sauce

SHOPPING LIST

PRODUCE

- ½ English cucumber
- 2 broccoli crowns
- 1 pound carrots
- 1 pound russet potatoes
- 1½ pounds zucchini
- 1 romaine lettuce heart
- 2 Roma tomatoes
- 1 medium white onion
- 1 jalapeño chile
- 1 large avocado
- 3 garlic cloves
- 1 bunch fresh flat-leaf parsley or dill
- 1 bunch fresh basil
- 1 bunch fresh cilantro
- 1 bunch fresh mint
- 1 lemon
- 2 limes

PANTRY

- 1 tablespoon za'atar
- 1½ teaspoons lemon pepper
- 1½ teaspoons ground cumin
- ½ teaspoon paprika
- ¼ teaspoon garlic salt
- ¼ teaspoon dried oregano
- ¼ teaspoon ground turmeric
- ½ cup mayonnaise
- ¼ cup red wine vinegar
- 1 teaspoon honey
- 1 small dill pickle
- 2 tablespoons capers
- ½ cup walnut halves and pieces
- 1½ cups long-grain white rice
- 1 pound penne pasta
- 4 pitas

DAIRY

- ½ cup plain whole-milk Greek yogurt
- 1 cup (4 ounces) shredded cheddar cheese
- ¾ cup grated parmesan cheese
- 4 tablespoons (½ stick) butter

PROTEIN

- 1½ pounds boneless, skinless chicken breast cutlets
- 2 pounds 90% lean ground beef
- 4 (6-ounce) cod fillets (about ¾ inch thick)

FROZEN

- 1 (1-pound) bag frozen peas

SUNDAY MEAL PREP RECIPES

no cook

pressure cooker

air fryer

oven

stovetop

microwave

Tartar Sauce

Makes about 1 cup

½ cup mayonnaise
1 small dill pickle, finely chopped
2 tablespoons capers, coarsely chopped
1½ tablespoons fresh chopped flat-leaf parsley or dill
2 tablespoons fresh lemon juice
⅛ teaspoon garlic powder
⅛ teaspoon ground black pepper

Add all the ingredients to a pint jar. Stir to combine. Label "Tartar Sauce" and store in the fridge.

Cucumber-Yogurt Sauce

Makes about 1 cup

½ English cucumber
½ cup plain whole-milk Greek yogurt
¼ teaspoon garlic salt (or ⅛ teaspoon garlic powder plus ¼ teaspoon kosher salt)

Grate the cucumber onto a cutting board, then use a knife to chop it up a bit further, so there aren't any long shreds.

Add the cucumber to a pint jar, along with the yogurt and garlic salt. Stir to combine. Label "Cucumber-Yogurt Sauce" and store in the fridge.

Broccoli Pesto

Makes about 2 cups

- 2 broccoli crowns, cut into 1-inch florets
- 1 bunch fresh basil leaves
- ¾ cup grated parmesan cheese
- ½ cup walnut halves and pieces
- 2 garlic cloves, peeled
- ½ teaspoon kosher salt
- ¼ teaspoon ground black pepper
- ½ cup olive oil

In a food processor, combine all the ingredients. Process in about 20 (1-second) pulses, stopping to scrape down the sides of the bowl as necessary, until the pesto is well processed.

Transfer the pesto to a pint jar. Label "Broccoli Pesto" and store in the fridge.

Taco Beef Seasoning Blend

Makes 1 batch

- 1 tablespoon chili powder
- 1½ teaspoons ground cumin
- ½ teaspoon paprika
- ¾ teaspoon kosher salt
- ¼ teaspoon garlic powder
- ¼ teaspoon onion powder
- ¼ teaspoon dried oregano

Add all the ingredients to a small jar or other lidded container. Stir to combine. Label "Taco Beef Seasoning Blend" and store at room temperature.

Carrot and Potato Prep

Makes 4 servings

- 1 pound carrots, peeled and cut into 2-inch pieces
- 1 pound russet potatoes, peeled and cut into 2-inch pieces

Put the carrots and potatoes in a lidded container or zip-top bag, label "Carrot and Potato Prep," and store in the fridge.

Zucchini Prep

Makes 4 servings

- 1½ pounds zucchini

With a crinkle cutter or knife, slice the zucchini into ½-inch-thick rounds. Transfer to a lidded container or zip-top bag, label "Zucchini Prep," and store in the fridge.

Lettuce Prep

Makes 4 servings

1 romaine lettuce heart, cut into 1-inch pieces

Put the lettuce in a lidded container or zip-top bag, label "Lettuce Prep," and store in the fridge.

Pico de Gallo

Makes about 1¼ cups

2 Roma tomatoes, cored and diced
¼ medium white onion, diced
1 jalapeño chile, seeded and diced
1 garlic clove, minced or pressed
3 fresh cilantro sprigs, chopped
1 tablespoon fresh lime juice
¼ teaspoon kosher salt

Add all the ingredients to a pint jar. Stir to combine. Label "Pico de Gallo" and store in the fridge.

Herb-Marinated Chicken Cutlets

Makes 4 servings

¼ cup olive oil
¼ cup red wine vinegar
1 teaspoon honey
1½ teaspoons Italian seasoning
½ teaspoon garlic powder
1¼ teaspoons kosher salt
1½ pounds boneless, skinless chicken breast cutlets

Place a large zip-top bag inside a wide-mouth pint jar with the top draped over. Add the oil, vinegar, honey, Italian seasoning, garlic powder, and salt. Remove the bag from the jar and use your hands to jostle the bag so the marinade ingredients are evenly combined. Add the chicken cutlets, seal the bag, pressing out as much air as possible, and jostle the bag around so the marinade evenly coats all the chicken. Label the bag "Herb-Marinated Chicken Cutlets" and store in the fridge.

No-Skewer Kabobs

Makes 4 servings

1 pound 90% lean ground beef
1 tablespoon onion powder
½ teaspoon garlic powder
¼ teaspoon ground turmeric
¼ teaspoon ground black pepper
¾ teaspoon kosher salt

Combine all the ingredients in a large bowl. Use your hands to knead the mixture until all the spices are evenly incorporated throughout the meat.

Divide the mixture into 8 equal pieces. Roll each piece into a 6-inch-long log, then use your fingers to flatten it into an approximately ½-inch-thick strip. Transfer to a lidded container, label "No-Skewer Kabobs," and store in the fridge.

Meal 1

Lemon Pepper Cod, Tartar Sauce, Minty Peas, Carrot and Potato Mash

Serves 4

- Carrot and Potato Prep (page 33)
- 4 tablespoons (½ stick) butter, divided
- Kosher salt and ground black pepper
- 4 (6-ounce) cod fillets (about ¾ inch thick)
- 1½ teaspoons lemon pepper
- 1 tablespoon chopped fresh flat-leaf parsley
- 1 (1-pound) bag frozen peas
- 1 tablespoon chopped fresh mint
- Tartar Sauce (page 31)

Pour a cup of water into the pressure cooker. Add the carrots and potatoes to a steamer basket and place it in the pot. Pressure-cook the vegetables for 4 minutes at **LOW** pressure, with a **QUICK** pressure release. Transfer the carrots and potatoes to a bowl. Add 1 tablespoon of the butter to the carrots and potatoes, along with salt and pepper to taste. Use a potato masher to mash the vegetables.

While the carrots and potatoes are cooking, preheat the air fryer to 375°F. Season the cod fillets with the lemon pepper, then dot them with 2 tablespoons butter (½ tablespoon per fillet). Add the cod in a single layer directly in the air fryer basket or on the baking sheet of an air fryer oven, lined with parchment paper or aluminum foil, and air-fry for 15 minutes. After cooking, sprinkle the fillets with the parsley.

Cook the peas according to the package instructions. In a serving bowl, combine them with the remaining 1 tablespoon butter and the mint, along with salt and pepper to taste. Stir to combine.

Transfer the mashed carrots and potatoes, cod, and peas to plates and serve right away, with tartar sauce on the side.

Meal 2

Ground Beef Burrito Bowls

Serves 4

- 1 tablespoon avocado oil or other neutral oil
- 1 pound 90% lean ground beef
- Taco Beef Seasoning Blend (page 32)
- 1½ cups long-grain white rice
- ½ teaspoon kosher salt
- 2 tablespoons chopped fresh cilantro
- Juice of 1 lime
- Lettuce Prep (page 34)
- Pico de Gallo (page 34)
- 1 cup (4 ounces) shredded cheddar cheese
- 1 large avocado, peeled, pitted, and cubed

Heat the oil in the pressure cooker on the **SAUTÉ** setting for a minute or two. Add the beef and sauté for about 5 minutes, until no pink remains. Stir in the taco seasoning blend and ½ cup water. Place a raised wire steam rack in the pot and place a 1½-quart stainless-steel bowl on the rack. Add the rice, salt, and 1½ cups water to the bowl. Pressure-cook for 10 minutes, with a 10-minute **NATURAL** pressure release.

Remove the bowl of rice and the steam rack. Add the cilantro and lime juice to the rice, then use a fork to mix and fluff the rice.

Transfer the rice and beef to serving bowls. Top with the romaine lettuce, pico de gallo, shredded cheese, and avocado. Serve right away.

Meal 3

Broccoli Pesto Penne with Italian Herb–Marinated Chicken Cutlets

Serves 4

1 pound penne pasta
Broccoli Pesto (page 32)
Herb-Marinated Chicken Cutlets (page 35)

Cook the pasta according to the package instructions. Drain the pasta and transfer it to a bowl. Add the broccoli pesto and stir to combine.

While the pasta is cooking, preheat the air fryer to 400°F. Add the chicken cutlets in a single layer directly in the air fryer basket or on the baking sheet of an air fryer oven, lined with parchment paper or aluminum foil, and air-fry for 15 minutes. (If using a basket-style air fryer, flip the cutlets after 10 minutes.)

Transfer the pasta and chicken to serving plates. Serve right away.

SERVE IT UP!

Meal 4

No-Skewer Kabobs, Za'atar Pitas, Herbed Zucchini Coins, Cucumber-Yogurt Sauce

Serves 4

No-Skewer Kabobs (page 35)
Zucchini Prep (page 33)
3 tablespoons olive oil, divided
2 tablespoons chopped fresh flat-leaf parsley
Kosher salt and ground black pepper
4 pitas
1 tablespoon za'atar
Cucumber-Yogurt Sauce (page 31)

Preheat the air fryer to 400°F. Add the kabobs in a single layer directly in the air fryer basket or on the baking sheet of an air fryer oven, lined with parchment paper or aluminum foil, and air-fry for 8 minutes. (If using a basket-style air fryer, flip the kabobs after 5 minutes.)

While the kabobs are cooking, pour a cup of water into the pressure cooker. Add the zucchini to a steamer basket and place it in the pot. Pressure-cook for 1 minute at **HIGH** pressure, with a **QUICK** pressure release. Toss the zucchini with 1 tablespoon of the olive oil, the parsley, and salt and pepper to taste.

Transfer the kabobs and zucchini to serving plates.

Place the pitas in the (now-empty) air fryer and brush them with the remaining 2 tablespoons olive oil. Air-fry for 3 minutes. Sprinkle the za'atar on the pitas, then transfer them to the serving plates with the kabobs and zucchini. Serve right away, with the cucumber-yogurt sauce on the side.

Week 3

SPICE AND CITRUS

Get ready for a week full of brightly flavored meals perked up with tangy ingredients like lemon juice, vinegar, and yogurt. First up is my girls' favorite fish, salmon. Here, it's seasoned with a Cajun spice blend, topped with a creamy lemon-dill sauce, and accompanied by broccoli-cheddar rice for veggies and a starchy side, all in one. Next up is a trip to the Mediterranean for a satisfying bowl of orzo topped with tender chicken meatballs and an herby tzatziki sauce. Enjoy lemony shrimp and rice pilaf on the third night, and lastly, a savory meal of steak bites and quinoa salad rounds out the week, served with a vinegary chimichurri.

Week 3 Menu

Cajun-Spiced Salmon Fillets, Lemon-Dill Sauce, Broccoli-Cheddar Rice

Greek-Inspired Chicken Meatballs, Spinach Orzo, Tzatziki

Italian-Spiced Shrimp, Lemony Rice Pilaf

Tri-Tip Steak Bites, Quinoa Salad with Roasted Bell Peppers, Chimichurri

SHOPPING LIST

PRODUCE

- 1 Persian cucumber or ½ English cucumber
- 2 green onions
- 1 head broccoli
- 1 (5- to 6-ounce) bag baby spinach
- 2 medium red bell peppers
- 1 medium yellow onion
- 4 garlic cloves
- 1 bunch fresh dill
- 1 bunch fresh flat-leaf parsley
- 3 lemons

PANTRY

- 2½ teaspoons dried oregano
- 1 teaspoon Cajun or Creole spice blend, such as Tony Chachere's
- 1 teaspoon lemon pepper
- ¾ teaspoon seasoned salt
- ¾ teaspoon red pepper flakes
- ¼ teaspoon paprika
- ¼ teaspoon garlic salt
- ⅛ teaspoon ground nutmeg
- 2 cups low-sodium vegetable or chicken broth
- ⅓ cup mayonnaise
- 3 tablespoons white wine vinegar
- 1 teaspoon Dijon mustard
- ½ cup panko breadcrumbs
- 1 cup quinoa
- 8 ounces orzo
- 2 cups long-grain white rice

DAIRY AND EGGS

- 1⅓ cups plain whole-milk Greek yogurt
- 1 cup (4 ounces) shredded sharp cheddar cheese
- 1 large egg

PROTEIN

- 1 pound 96% lean ground chicken
- 1½ pounds tri-tip roast or steaks
- 4 (6-ounce) salmon fillets (about ¾ inch thick)

FROZEN

- 1 pound frozen large peeled and deveined shrimp

SUNDAY MEAL PREP RECIPES

no cook

pressure cooker

air fryer

oven

stovetop

microwave

Lemon-Dill Sauce

Makes about ¾ cup

⅓ cup mayonnaise
⅓ cup plain whole-milk Greek yogurt
Grated zest and juice of ½ lemon
2 tablespoons chopped fresh dill
¼ teaspoon garlic powder
¼ teaspoon kosher salt

Add all the ingredients to a pint jar. Stir to combine, label "Lemon-Dill Sauce," and store in the fridge.

Tzatziki

Makes about 1⅓ cups

1 cup plain whole-milk Greek yogurt
1 Persian cucumber (or ½ English cucumber), grated on a coarse grater
1 garlic clove, minced or pressed
1 tablespoon olive oil
Grated zest and juice of ½ lemon
1 tablespoon chopped fresh dill
½ teaspoon kosher salt
¼ teaspoon ground black pepper

Add all the ingredients to a pint jar. Stir to combine, label "Tzatziki," and store in the fridge.

Chimichurri

Makes about 1 cup

- 3 large garlic cloves, peeled
- 1 loosely packed cup fresh flat-leaf parsley leaves and tender stems
- 2 green onions, trimmed
- ⅓ cup olive oil
- 3 tablespoons white wine vinegar
- 1 teaspoon kosher salt
- 1 teaspoon dried oregano
- ½ teaspoon red pepper flakes (optional)
- ½ teaspoon ground black pepper

Pile the garlic, parsley, and green onions on a cutting board. Chop them together until everything is finely chopped and uniform. Transfer the mixture to a pint jar.

Add the oil, vinegar, salt, oregano, red pepper flakes (if using), and black pepper to the jar. Stir to combine, label "Chimichurri," and store in the fridge.

Greek-Inspired Chicken Meatball Mixture

Makes 4 servings (about 20 meatballs)

- 1 pound 96% lean ground chicken
- 1 large egg
- Grated zest and juice of 1 lemon
- ½ cup panko breadcrumbs
- 1½ teaspoons dried oregano
- ¾ teaspoon garlic powder
- ¼ teaspoon ground black pepper
- ⅛ teaspoon ground nutmeg
- ¾ teaspoon kosher salt

Combine all the ingredients in a large bowl. Use your hands to mix everything together until well combined. Transfer to a tightly lidded container, label "Greek-Inspired Chicken Meatball Mixture," and store in the fridge.

Italian-Spiced Shrimp Marinade

Makes about ¼ cup (for 1 pound shrimp)

2 tablespoons olive oil
Grated zest and juice of ½ lemon
¾ teaspoon Italian seasoning
½ teaspoon garlic powder
¼ teaspoon red pepper flakes
¼ teaspoon paprika
½ teaspoon kosher salt

Add all the ingredients to a small jar or lidded container. Shake to combine, label "Italian-Spiced Shrimp Marinade," and store in the fridge.

Tri-Tip Steak Bites

Serves 4

1 tablespoon avocado oil or other neutral oil
1 teaspoon Dijon mustard
1 teaspoon lemon pepper
1 teaspoon garlic powder
¾ teaspoon seasoned salt
1½ pounds tri-tip roast or steaks, cut into 1½-inch pieces

In a large bowl, combine the oil, mustard, lemon pepper, garlic powder, and seasoned salt to make a thick paste. Add the steak and mix with your hands to evenly coat all the pieces with the seasoning paste. Transfer to a zip-top bag or tightly lidded container, label "Tri-Tip Steak Bites," and store in the fridge.

Broccoli Prep

Makes 4 servings

1 head broccoli, trimmed and cut into 1-inch florets

Put the broccoli florets in a lidded container or zip-top bag, label "Broccoli Prep," and store in the fridge.

Cooked Quinoa

Makes about 3 cups

1 cup quinoa
¼ teaspoon kosher salt

Pour 1 cup water into the pressure cooker. Place a raised wire steam rack in the pot, and place a 1½-quart stainless-steel bowl on the rack. Add the quinoa, salt, and another 1 cup water to the bowl. Pressure-cook for 8 minutes at **HIGH** pressure, with a 10-minute **NATURAL** pressure release.

Transfer the quinoa to a sheet pan, fluffing it with a fork and spreading it into an even layer. Let cool to room temperature, about 20 minutes, then transfer to a lidded container, label "Cooked Quinoa," and store in the fridge.

Spinach Orzo

Makes 4 servings

8 ounces (1¼ cups) orzo
2 cups low-sodium vegetable or chicken broth
1 tablespoon olive oil
1 (5- to 6-ounce) bag baby spinach

Add the orzo, broth, and olive oil to the pressure cooker. Pressure-cook the orzo for 5 minutes at **HIGH** pressure, with a **QUICK** pressure release. Stir in the baby spinach, let sit for 2 minutes, then stir again—the spinach should have wilted down from the heat of the pasta. Let cool to room temperature, transfer to a tightly lidded container, label "Spinach Orzo," and store in the fridge.

10.

Steamed Long-Grain White Rice

Makes 6 cups

- 2 cups long-grain white rice
- ½ teaspoon kosher salt

Add the rice, salt, and 2 cups water to the pressure cooker. Pressure-cook on the Rice setting (or for 12 minutes at **LOW** pressure), with a 10-minute **NATURAL** pressure release.

Transfer the rice to a sheet pan, fluffing it with a fork and spreading it into an even layer. Let cool to room temperature, about 20 minutes, then divide in half and transfer to two lidded containers or zip-top bags. Label the containers "Steamed Long-Grain White Rice for Broccoli-Cheddar Rice" and "Steamed Long-Grain White Rice for Lemony Rice Pilaf" and store in the fridge.

11.

Roasted Peppers and Onion

Makes 4 servings

- 2 medium red bell peppers, seeded and cut into 1-inch strips
- 1 medium yellow onion, cut into 1-inch strips
- 1 tablespoon olive oil
- ¼ teaspoon kosher salt

Preheat the air fryer to 400°F. In a bowl, toss the peppers and onion with the olive oil and salt. Arrange the vegetables in a single layer directly in the air fryer basket or on the baking sheet of an air fryer oven, lined with parchment paper or aluminum foil, and air-fry for 10 minutes. Cool to room temperature, transfer to a tightly lidded container, label "Roasted Peppers and Onion," and store in the fridge.

Meal 1

Cajun-Spiced Salmon Fillets, Lemon-Dill Sauce, Broccoli-Cheddar Rice

Serves 4

- Broccoli Prep (page 51)
- Steamed Long-Grain White Rice for Broccoli-Cheddar Rice (page 53)
- 1 cup (4 ounces) shredded sharp cheddar cheese
- 4 (6-ounce) salmon fillets (about ¾ inch thick)
- 1 teaspoon Cajun or Creole spice blend, such as Tony Chachere's (or Old Bay for a mild alternative)
- Lemon-Dill Sauce (page 47)

Pour a cup of water into the pressure cooker. Add the broccoli florets to a steamer basket and place it in the pot. Pressure-cook for 0 (zero) minutes at **LOW** pressure, with a **QUICK** pressure release. (If your pressure cooker does not have a setting for 0 minutes, set it for 1 minute, then perform a **QUICK** pressure release right when the cooking program begins its countdown.) Remove the steamer basket from the pot, pour out the water, then return the broccoli to the warm pot, along with the steamed rice and shredded cheese. Stir to combine, then leave on the Keep Warm setting.

While the broccoli is steaming, preheat the air fryer to 375°F. Season the salmon fillets with the Cajun spice blend. Add the salmon in a single layer directly in the air fryer basket or on the baking sheet of an air fryer oven, lined with parchment paper or aluminum foil, and air-fry for 10 minutes. Use a fork to test a piece of salmon for doneness—if it flakes easily, it is cooked through. If not, air-fry for a few minutes longer.

Transfer the rice and salmon to serving plates. Serve right away, with the lemon-dill sauce on the side.

Meal 2

Greek-Inspired Chicken Meatballs, Spinach Orzo, Tzatziki

Serves 4

Greek-Inspired Chicken Meatball Mixture (page 48)
Spinach Orzo (page 52)
Tzatziki (page 47)

Preheat the air fryer to 400°F. Use a 1½-tablespoon scoop to portion out the meatballs directly into the air fryer basket or onto the baking sheet of an air fryer oven, lined with parchment paper or aluminum foil. Air-fry for 10 minutes.

While the meatballs are cooking, reheat the orzo in a microwave-safe bowl in the microwave for 3½ minutes, stirring once halfway through.

Transfer the meatballs and orzo to serving plates or bowls. Serve right away, with the tzatziki on the side.

Meal 3

Italian-Spiced Shrimp, Lemony Rice Pilaf

Serves 4

- 1 pound frozen large peeled and deveined shrimp, thawed according to package instructions
- Italian-Spiced Shrimp Marinade (page 50)
- 1 tablespoon olive oil
- Steamed Long-Grain White Rice (page 53)
- ¼ teaspoon garlic salt
- Grated zest and juice of ½ lemon
- 1 tablespoon chopped fresh flat-leaf parsley

In a bowl, toss the shrimp with the marinade. Preheat the air fryer to 400°F.

Meanwhile, heat the oil in the pressure cooker on the **SAUTÉ** setting for a minute or so. Add the rice and garlic salt and sauté until warmed through. Stir in the lemon zest, lemon juice, and parsley. Turn off the heat.

Add the shrimp in a single layer directly in the air fryer basket or on the baking sheet of an air fryer oven, lined with parchment paper or aluminum foil, and air-fry for 4 minutes.

Transfer the rice pilaf and shrimp to serving plates. Serve right away.

NOTE: I like to serve this meal with a no-cook vegetable side, such as a caprese salad or a plate of sliced cucumbers and whole cherry tomatoes, dressed with balsamic vinegar, olive oil, salt, and pepper.

Meal 4

Tri-Tip Steak Bites, Quinoa Salad with Roasted Bell Peppers, Chimichurri

Serves 4

- Tri-Tip Steak Bites (page 50)
- Cooked Quinoa (page 51)
- Roasted Peppers and Onion (page 53)
- Chimichurri (page 48), divided

Preheat the air fryer to 400°F. Add the steak bites in a single layer directly in the air fryer basket or on the baking sheet of an air fryer oven, lined with parchment paper or aluminum foil, and air-fry for 8 minutes.

While the steak bites are cooking, toss the quinoa with the roasted peppers and onion and ⅓ cup of the chimichurri.

Transfer the quinoa salad and steak bites to serving plates and serve right away, with the remaining chimichurri on the side.

Week 4
GLOBAL COMFORTS

Let's take a trip around the world and explore a pantry full of flavors. Olives and capers add their briny flavors to roasted cod—the tomato relish acts as both a condiment and a vegetable accompaniment. Sloppy joes are filled with a Latin American–style picadillo and served with a crunchy and refreshing salad. Next, enjoy Hawaiian-inspired chicken thighs in a ginger-spiked marinade, alongside savory roasted green beans and fluffy jasmine rice. Rounding out the week there's a kid-friendly and simple pasta dish: orecchiette (or your favorite short pasta) tossed with mini meatballs and peas.

Week 4 Menu

Roasted Cod with Tomato and Olive Relish, Herbed Baby Potatoes

Picadillo Joes, Jicama and Orange Salad

Soy-Ginger Chicken Thighs, Jasmine Rice, Steamed Green Beans

Orecchiette with Turkey Meatballs and Peas

SHOPPING LIST

PRODUCE

- 1½ pounds petite gold or red potatoes (2 inches or less in diameter)
- 1 pound green beans
- 3 green onions
- 2 Roma tomatoes
- 1 medium jicama
- 1 medium yellow onion
- 1 large red bell pepper
- 3 garlic cloves
- 1 bunch fresh flat-leaf parsley
- 2 oranges
- 1 lemon

PANTRY

- ¼ cup brown sugar
- 1 teaspoon ground cumin
- 1 teaspoon lemon pepper
- ½ teaspoon garlic salt
- 1 teaspoon ground ginger
- ¼ teaspoon dried oregano
- 2 bay leaves
- 4 cups low-sodium chicken or vegetable broth
- ½ cup pineapple juice
- ⅓ cup pitted kalamata olives
- ¼ cup soy sauce
- ¼ cup ketchup
- ¼ cup tomato paste
- 1 tablespoon red wine vinegar
- 2 teaspoons agave nectar
- 4 kaiser rolls
- 1 (1-pound) package orecchiette
- ½ cup panko breadcrumbs
- 1½ cups jasmine rice

DAIRY AND EGGS

- ½ cup grated parmesan cheese
- 1 large egg

MEAT AND PROTEIN

- 1½ pounds boneless, skinless chicken thighs
- 1 pound 93% lean ground turkey
- 1 pound 90% lean ground beef
- 4 (6-ounce) cod fillets (about ¾ inch thick)

FROZEN

- 1 (1-pound) bag frozen peas

SUNDAY MEAL PREP RECIPES

no cook

pressure cooker

air fryer

oven

stovetop

microwave

Tomato and Olive Relish

Makes about 1 cup

2 Roma tomatoes, cored and diced
⅓ cup pitted kalamata olives, roughly chopped
2 green onions, chopped
1 garlic clove, minced or pressed
2 tablespoons olive oil
1 tablespoon red wine vinegar
¼ teaspoon dried oregano
¼ teaspoon kosher salt
⅛ teaspoon ground black pepper

In a bowl, stir together all the ingredients until evenly combined. Transfer to a pint jar, label "Tomato and Olive Relish," and store in the fridge.

Gremolata

Makes about ⅓ cup

1 (loosely packed) cup fresh flat-leaf parsley leaves
2 garlic cloves, peeled
Coarsely grated zest of 1 large lemon (reserve the lemon to juice for the Cumin-Lemon Vinaigrette)

Pile the parsley and garlic on a cutting board. Chop them together until the garlic is uniformly minced and combined with the parsley. Add the lemon zest and chop a little more, until everything is well combined. Transfer to a small jar or other tightly lidded container, label "Gremolata," and store in the fridge.

Cumin-Lemon Vinaigrette

Makes about ½ cup

Juice of 1 large lemon
¼ cup avocado oil or other neutral oil
2 teaspoons agave nectar
½ teaspoon kosher salt
¼ teaspoon ground cumin

Add all the ingredients to a half-pint jar or other small, lidded container. Shake well to combine, label "Cumin-Lemon Vinaigrette," and store in the fridge.

Soy-Ginger Chicken Thighs

Makes 4 servings

1½ pounds boneless, skinless chicken thighs
½ cup pineapple juice
¼ cup soy sauce
¼ cup ketchup
¼ cup brown sugar
1 teaspoon ground ginger
1 teaspoon garlic powder

Add the chicken thighs to a lidded container or zip-top bag.

In a bowl, stir together the pineapple juice, soy sauce, ketchup, brown sugar, ginger, and garlic powder. Pour the mixture over the chicken, then use tongs to toss the chicken in the marinade until all of the thighs are coated. Label "Soy-Ginger Chicken Thighs," and store in the fridge.

5.

Turkey Meatball Mixture

Makes 4 servings

1 pound 93% lean ground turkey

½ cup panko breadcrumbs

1 large egg

½ teaspoon Italian seasoning

½ teaspoon kosher salt

Combine all of the ingredients in a large bowl. Use your hands to mix everything together until well combined. Transfer to a tightly lidded container, label "Turkey Meatball Mixture," and store in the fridge.

6.

Jicama and Orange Prep

Makes 4 servings

1 medium jicama, cut into ¼-inch-thick matchsticks

2 oranges, peeled

Cut the jicama into ¼-inch-thick matchsticks. Transfer to a lidded container or zip-top bag, label "Jicama Prep," and store in the fridge. Supreme the oranges (or just cut them up into bite-size pieces, if you don't mind eating the membranes). Transfer to a separate lidded container or zip-top bag, label "Orange Prep," and store in the fridge.

Green Bean Prep

Makes 4 servings

1 pound green beans, trimmed

Put the green beans in a lidded container or zip-top bag, label "Green Bean Prep," and store in the fridge.

Picadillo and Jasmine Rice

Makes 4 servings

FOR THE RICE

1½ cups jasmine rice

¼ teaspoon kosher salt

FOR THE PICADILLO

1 pound 90% lean ground beef

1 medium yellow onion, diced

1 large red bell pepper, seeded and diced

1 teaspoon garlic powder

¾ teaspoon ground cumin

½ teaspoon kosher salt

¼ teaspoon ground black pepper

2 bay leaves

¼ cup tomato paste

Add the rice, salt, and 1¾ cups water to a 1½-quart stainless-steel bowl and set aside.

Select the pressure cooker's **SAUTÉ** setting and add the ground beef. **SAUTÉ**, breaking the beef up with a spoon as it cooks, for about 5 minutes, until the meat is no longer pink. Add the onion and bell pepper and sauté for about 3 more minutes, until the onion begins to soften. Add the garlic powder, cumin, salt, pepper, bay leaves, and ½ cup water and stir to combine. Add the tomato paste in a dollop on top—do not stir it in.

Add a raised wire steam rack to the pressure cooker. Place the bowl with the rice on the steam rack.

Pressure-cook for 10 minutes at **HIGH** pressure, with a 10-minute **NATURAL** pressure release.

Transfer the rice to a sheet pan, fluffing it with a fork and spreading it into an even layer. Transfer the picadillo to a lidded container, label "Picadillo," and store in the fridge. Let the rice cool to room temperature, about 20 minutes, then transfer to a separate lidded container, label "Jasmine Rice," and store in the fridge.

Meal 1

Roasted Cod with Tomato and Olive Relish, Herbed Baby Potatoes

Serves 4

1½ pounds petite gold or red potatoes (2 inches or less in diameter)
2 tablespoons olive oil
Gremolata (page 65)
4 (6-ounce) cod fillets (about ¾ inch thick)
1 teaspoon lemon pepper
½ teaspoon garlic salt
Avocado oil spray
Tomato and Olive Relish (page 65)

Pour a cup of water into the pressure cooker. Add the potatoes to a steamer basket and place it in the cooker. Pressure-cook for 5 minutes at **HIGH** pressure, with a **QUICK** pressure release. Remove the steamer basket, pour out the water, then return the potatoes to the pot, along with the olive oil and gremolata. Stir to combine, then leave on the Keep Warm setting.

While the potatoes are cooking, preheat the air fryer to 375°F. Season the cod fillets with the lemon pepper and garlic salt, then spray them lightly with avocado oil spray. Add the cod in a single layer directly in the air fryer basket or on the baking sheet of an air fryer oven, lined with parchment paper or aluminum foil, and air-fry for 15 minutes.

Transfer the potatoes and cod to serving plates and serve right away, with the tomato and olive relish on the side

Meal 2

Picadillo Joes, Jicama and Orange Salad

Serves 4

- Picadillo (page 69)
- Jicama and Orange Prep (page 67)
- Cumin-Lemon Vinaigrette (page 66)
- 4 kaiser rolls

Warm the picadillo in a microwave-safe bowl in the microwave for about 5 minutes, stirring halfway through.

In a bowl, toss together the jicama, oranges, and vinaigrette.

Place the kaiser rolls, opened, on serving plates and ladle on the picadillo to make sandwiches. It's okay if some of the picadillo spills out—they're joes, after all! Serve right away, with the jicama and orange salad on the side.

Meal 3

Soy-Ginger Chicken Thighs, Jasmine Rice, Steamed Green Beans

Serves 4

Green Bean Prep (page 68)
Soy-Ginger Chicken Thighs (page 66)
Jasmine Rice (page 69)
1 green onion

Pour a cup of water into the pressure cooker. Add the green beans to a steamer basket and place it in the pressure cooker. Pressure-cook for 2 minutes at **LOW** pressure, with a **QUICK** pressure release. Leave them on the Keep Warm setting.

While the green beans are steaming, preheat the air fryer to 400°F. Add the chicken thighs in a single layer directly in the air fryer basket or on the baking sheet of an air fryer oven, lined with parchment paper or aluminum foil, and air-fry for 15 minutes, until they are cooked through and browned.

Reheat the jasmine rice in a microwave-safe bowl in the microwave for 2 minutes, stirring once halfway through.

Transfer the green beans, chicken, and rice to serving plates and serve right away, with the green onion snipped over the top of the chicken and rice to garnish.

Meal 4

Orecchiette with Turkey Meatballs and Peas

Serves 4 to 6

- 1 (1-pound) package orecchiette
- 4 cups low-sodium chicken or vegetable broth
- 1 tablespoon olive oil
- Turkey Meatball Mixture (page 67)
- 1 (1-pound) bag frozen peas (no need to thaw)
- Grated parmesan cheese, for serving
- Freshly ground black pepper, for serving

Add the pasta, broth, and olive oil to the pressure cooker. Pressure-cook for 5 minutes at **HIGH** pressure, with a 5-minute **NATURAL** pressure release.

While the pasta is cooking, preheat the air fryer to 400°F. Use a 1½-tablespoon scoop to portion out the meatballs directly into the air fryer basket or onto the baking sheet of an air fryer oven, lined with parchment paper or aluminum foil. Air-fry for 10 minutes.

Open the pressure cooker and stir the peas and meatballs into the pasta. Let sit for 2 minutes, then stir again.

Spoon the pasta, meatballs, and peas into serving bowls and serve right away, with parmesan cheese and black pepper for sprinkling on top.

Week 5
FUSION FIESTA

Monday's meal is a Mexican-inspired (and dairy-free) mac 'n' cheese served alongside a mix of roasted zucchini and tomatoes. Tuesday takes things to the Mediterranean with a simple yet flavorful meal of pork tenderloin, potatoes, and asparagus, all of which are delicious paired with the Spanish-inspired paprika aioli. Vietnamese flavors take the stage on Wednesday, with a noodle bowl including meatballs, fresh and crunchy cucumber, and a plussed-up sauce that balances sweetness, acid, salt, and a little bit of spicy heat. Finally, a one-pot dish ends the week: a creamy, satisfying artichoke-spinach pasta.

Week 5 Menu

Mac 'n' Queso (dairy-free), Zesty Zucchini and Tomatoes

Spanish-Style Pork Tenderloin and Potatoes, Steamed Asparagus, Paprika Aioli

Vietnamese-Inspired Chicken Meatball Noodle Bowls, Nước Chấm Plus

Artichoke-Spinach Pasta

SHOPPING LIST

PRODUCE

- 1½ pounds petite gold potatoes (2 inches or less in diameter)
- 1 pound asparagus
- 1 (8-ounce) Yukon gold potato
- 1 pint cherry tomatoes
- 1 large zucchini
- 1 medium yellow onion
- 1 large carrot
- 1 English cucumber
- 6 jalapeño chiles
- 4 green onions
- 7 garlic cloves
- 1 bunch fresh cilantro
- 2 large limes

PANTRY

- ¼ cup plus 1½ teaspoons organic cane sugar
- 2½ teaspoons paprika
- 2 teaspoons dried oregano
- 2 teaspoons nutritional yeast
- 1 teaspoon garlic salt
- ½ teaspoon ground ginger
- ¼ teaspoon ground cumin
- ⅛ teaspoon ground turmeric
- ¼ cup raw cashews (whole or pieces)
- 9 cups low-sodium chicken or vegetable broth
- 1 (12-ounce) jar marinated artichoke hearts
- ½ cup mayonnaise
- 3 tablespoons fish sauce
- 1 tablespoon soy sauce
- 1 tablespoon white wine vinegar
- 1 teaspoon sambal oelek or sriracha, plus more for serving
- 1 pound elbow macaroni
- 1 pound penne pasta
- 1 (8.8-ounce) package rice vermicelli noodles (such as Thai Kitchen or A Taste of Thai)
- ½ cup panko breadcrumbs

DAIRY AND EGGS

- 4 ounces cream cheese
- ½ cup plain whole-milk Greek yogurt
- ¾ cup (3 ounces) shredded mozzarella cheese
- ½ cup grated parmesan cheese, plus more for serving
- 1 large egg

MEAT AND PROTEIN

- 1 pound (96% lean) ground chicken
- 1 (1¼- to 1½-pound) pork tenderloin

FROZEN

- 1 (8-ounce) package frozen chopped spinach

SUNDAY MEAL PREP RECIPES

no cook

pressure cooker

air fryer

oven

stovetop

microwave

1.

Zesty Zucchini and Tomato Prep

Makes 4 servings

1 large zucchini, trimmed
½ medium yellow onion, diced
2 jalapeño chiles, diced
1 pint cherry tomatoes

Crinkle cut or slice the zucchini into ¼-inch-thick rounds. Put the zucchini, onion, jalapeños, and cherry tomatoes in a lidded container or zip-top bag. Label "Zesty Zucchini and Tomato Prep" and store in the fridge.

2.

Asparagus Prep

Makes 4 servings

1 pound asparagus

Trim the tough bottom few inches off the asparagus spears. Transfer the spears to a lidded container or zip-top bag, label "Asparagus Prep," and store in the fridge.

Cucumber and Cilantro Prep

Makes 4 servings

- 1 English cucumber, trimmed and sliced into ¼-inch-thick rounds
- 12 fresh cilantro sprigs

Put the cucumber and cilantro in a lidded container or zip-top bag, label "Cucumber and Cilantro Prep," and store in the fridge.

Paprika Aioli

Makes about ½ cup

- ½ cup mayonnaise
- 3 garlic cloves, peeled
- 1 teaspoon paprika

Combine all the ingredients in a wide-mouth pint jar. Lower an immersion blender into the jar and blend at **HIGH** speed for about 30 seconds, until smooth. (Alternatively, blend all the ingredients in a countertop blender, then transfer to a jar.) Label "Paprika Aioli" and store in the fridge.

Nước Chấm Plus

Makes about 1 cup

¼ cup organic cane sugar
¼ cup water
1 jalapeño chile, seeded and finely diced
2 green onions, chopped
1 garlic clove, minced or pressed
2 tablespoons fish sauce
1 tablespoon chopped fresh cilantro
Juice of 1 large lime

Combine all the ingredients in a pint jar. Shake to combine. Label "Nước Chấm Plus" and store in the fridge.

Artichoke-Spinach Pasta Sauce

Makes 1 batch (for 1 pound of pasta)

4 ounces cream cheese, at room temperature
½ cup plain whole-milk Greek yogurt
1 teaspoon Italian seasoning
½ teaspoon garlic powder
¼ teaspoon ground black pepper
¾ cup (3 ounces) shredded mozzarella cheese
½ cup grated parmesan cheese
1 (12-ounce) jar marinated artichoke hearts, drained and chopped
1 (8-ounce) package frozen chopped spinach (no need to thaw)

In a large bowl, stir together the cream cheese, yogurt, Italian seasoning, garlic powder, and pepper until well combined. Add the mozzarella, parmesan, artichoke hearts, and spinach and stir to combine. Transfer to a lidded container, label "Artichoke-Spinach Pasta Sauce," and store in the fridge.

7.

Chicken Meatball Mixture

Serves 4

1 pound (96% lean) ground chicken
1 large egg
½ cup panko breadcrumbs
1 tablespoon fish sauce
1 tablespoon soy sauce
1 tablespoon lime juice
1½ teaspoons organic cane sugar
1 teaspoon sambal oelek or sriracha
½ teaspoon ground ginger
2 garlic cloves, minced or pressed
2 green onions, chopped
1 jalapeño chile, seeded and diced

Combine all the ingredients in a large bowl. Use your hands to mix everything together until well combined. Transfer to a tightly lidded container, label "Chicken Meatball Mixture," and store in the fridge.

8.

Spanish-Style Pork Tenderloin

Serves 4

1 tablespoon olive oil
1 tablespoon white wine vinegar
1½ teaspoons paprika
1½ teaspoons dried oregano
1½ teaspoons kosher salt
½ teaspoon ground black pepper
¼ teaspoon ground cumin
1 (1¼- to 1½-pound) pork tenderloin

In a small bowl, combine the oil, vinegar, paprika, oregano, salt, pepper, and cumin to make a thick paste. Add the pork and mix with your hands to evenly coat it with the seasoning paste. Transfer to a zip-top bag or tightly lidded container, label "Spanish-Style Pork Tenderloin," and store in the fridge.

9.

Queso Sauce

Makes about 2½ cups (enough for 1 pound of pasta)

1 tablespoon avocado oil or other neutral oil
1 garlic clove, minced or pressed
½ medium yellow onion, diced
2 jalapeño chiles, seeded and diced
½ teaspoon kosher salt
½ teaspoon chili powder
⅛ teaspoon ground turmeric
1 cup vegetable broth
1 (8-ounce) Yukon Gold potato, peeled and diced
1 large carrot, peeled and cut into 1-inch chunks
¼ cup raw cashews (whole or pieces), chopped
2 teaspoons nutritional yeast
1 tablespoon fresh lime juice

Heat the oil and garlic in the pressure cooker on the **SAUTÉ** setting until the garlic is bubbling but not browned, about 1 minute. Add the onion and jalapeños and sauté for 3 minutes, until the onion is a bit softened. Add the salt, chili powder, and turmeric and stir for a few seconds, until fragrant. Stir in the broth, potato, carrot, and cashews. Pressure-cook for 1 minute at **HIGH** pressure, with a 10-minute **NATURAL** pressure release.

Transfer everything to a blender, add the nutritional yeast and lime juice, and blend until smooth, about 1 minute. Taste for seasoning, adding more salt if needed. Transfer to a quart jar or other lidded container and let cool to room temperature. Label "Queso Sauce" and store in the fridge.

Meal 1

Mac 'n' Queso (dairy-free), Zesty Zucchini and Tomatoes

Serves 4

- 1 pound elbow macaroni
- 4 cups low-sodium chicken or vegetable broth
- Queso Sauce (page 85)
- Zesty Zucchini and Tomato Prep (page 81)
- 1 tablespoon olive oil
- ½ teaspoon dried oregano
- ½ teaspoon garlic salt

In the pressure cooker, combine the macaroni and broth. Pressure-cook for 5 minutes at **HIGH** pressure, with a 5-minute **NATURAL** pressure release. Open the pot, stir in the queso sauce, and let sit on the Keep Warm setting until ready to serve.

While the macaroni is cooking, preheat the air fryer to 375°F. In a bowl, toss the zucchini and tomato mixture with the olive oil, oregano, and garlic salt. Add the mixture directly to the basket of an air fryer or on the baking sheet of an air fryer oven, lined with parchment paper or aluminum foil, and air-fry for 10 minutes.

Transfer the macaroni and veggies to serving plates and serve right away.

NOTE: I love serving watermelon wedges alongside this meal in the summertime.

Meal 2

Spanish-Style Pork Tenderloin and Potatoes, Steamed Asparagus, Paprika Aioli

Serves 4

- Spanish-Style Pork Tenderloin (page 84)
- 1½ pounds petite gold potatoes (2 inches or less in diameter)
- 1 tablespoon olive oil
- ½ teaspoon garlic salt
- Asparagus Prep (page 81)
- Paprika Aioli (page 82)

Preheat the air fryer to 350°F. Add the pork tenderloin and potatoes in a single layer directly in the air fryer basket or to the baking sheet of an air fryer oven, lined with parchment paper or aluminum foil. Drizzle the potatoes with the olive oil and sprinkle on the garlic salt. Air-fry for 30 minutes, or until the pork measures 145°F in the center when measured with an instant-read thermometer.

When the pork has about 10 minutes left to cook, add a cup of water to the pressure cooker and place a wire steam rack in the pot. Add the asparagus, then pressure-cook for 1 minute at **LOW** pressure, with a **QUICK** pressure release.

Slice the pork into ½-inch-thick medallions. Transfer it to serving plates, along with the potatoes and asparagus. Serve right away, with the paprika aioli on the side.

Meal 3

Vietnamese-Inspired Chicken Meatball Noodle Bowls, Nước Chấm Plus

Serves 4

- 1 (8.8-ounce) package rice vermicelli noodles
- Chicken Meatball Mixture (page 84)
- Cucumber and Cilantro Prep (page 82)
- Nước Chấm Plus (page 83)

Prepare the noodles according to the package instructions, by either boiling or soaking in hot water, then rinsing in cold water. Leave to drain in a colander.

Preheat the air fryer to 400°F. Use a 1½-tablespoon scoop to portion out chicken meatballs directly into the air fryer basket or onto the baking sheet of an air fryer oven, lined with parchment paper or aluminum foil. Air-fry for 10 minutes.

Transfer the noodles and meatballs to serving bowls, tucking in the cucumber and cilantro on the side of the bowl. Serve right away, with the nước chấm plus on the side.

Meal 4

Artichoke-Spinach Pasta

Serves 4

- 1 pound penne pasta
- 4 cups low-sodium chicken or vegetable broth
- Artichoke-Spinach Pasta Sauce (page 83)
- Grated parmesan cheese, for serving

In the pressure cooker, combine the pasta and broth. Pressure-cook for 5 minutes at **HIGH** pressure, with a 5-minute **NATURAL** pressure release. Open the pot, stir in the artichoke-spinach pasta sauce, let stand for 2 minutes, then stir once more. Let sit on the Keep Warm setting until ready to serve.

Spoon the pasta into serving bowls and serve right away, with parmesan cheese on the side.

Week 6

SPICE ROUTE

What family doesn't enjoy a big pot of spaghetti and some toasty, cheese-topped garlic bread? Here, some extra vegetables are blended into the sauce, along with a pound of ground beef. On the next night, Indian-inspired flavors are the star of a vegetarian menu, with a cilantro chutney that perks up warmly spiced bites of tofu and basmati rice with green beans mixed right in. Wednesday brings my favorite Moroccan spice blend, ras el hanout, to a plate of turkey meatballs and couscous cooked with grated carrots. Thursday rounds out the meal plan with an easy dish of sausage, okra, and peppers served over buttered basmati rice.

Week 6 Menu

Supercharged Spaghetti, Cheesy Garlic Toast

Green Bean Rice, Masala Tofu Bites, Cilantro Chutney

Moroccan-Spiced Turkey Meatballs, Carrot Pearl Couscous

Sausage, Okra, and Peppers, Buttered Rice

SHOPPING LIST

PRODUCE

- 8 ounces green beans
- 4 large carrots
- 2 medium yellow onions
- 2 red bell peppers
- 1 large zucchini
- 1 jalapeño chile
- 7 garlic cloves
- 1 bunch fresh cilantro
- 1 bunch fresh flat-leaf parsley
- 2 large limes
- 1 lemon

PANTRY

- 1 tablespoon nutritional yeast
- 1 tablespoon cornstarch
- 2 teaspoons garam masala
- 1 teaspoon ras el hanout
- ½ teaspoon cumin seeds
- ¼ teaspoon paprika
- ¼ teaspoon ground cumin
- ⅛ teaspoon cayenne pepper (optional)
- 5½ cups low-sodium chicken or vegetable broth
- 1 (14-ounce) can petite diced tomatoes
- 1 (6-ounce) can tomato paste
- 8 ounces spaghetti
- 8 ounces (1¼ cups) pearl or Israeli couscous
- 2 cups basmati rice
- ½ cup plain breadcrumbs
- ½ cup raw cashews (whole or pieces)
- 1 loaf crusty Italian bread

DAIRY AND EGGS

- ½ cup plain whole-milk Greek yogurt
- ¼ cup grated parmesan cheese, plus more for serving
- 4 tablespoons (½ stick) butter
- 1 large egg

MEAT AND PROTEIN

- 1 (14- to 16-ounce) package extra-firm tofu
- 1 pound 93% lean ground turkey
- 1 (12-ounce) link Polish pork kielbasa
- 1 pound 90% lean ground beef

FROZEN

- 1 (12-ounce) package frozen cut okra

SUNDAY MEAL PREP RECIPES

no cook

pressure cooker

air fryer

oven

stovetop

microwave

1.

Garlic Toast Spread

Serves 4 (for 4 pieces of bread)

2 tablespoons butter, at room temperature
¼ cup grated parmesan cheese
2 garlic cloves, minced or pressed
½ teaspoon Italian seasoning
¼ teaspoon paprika

In a small lidded container, mix the butter, cheese, garlic, Italian seasoning, and paprika until thoroughly combined. Label "Garlic Toast Spread" and store in the fridge.

2.

Masala Marinated Tofu

Serves 4

1 tablespoon nutritional yeast
1 tablespoon cornstarch
2 teaspoons garam masala
¼ teaspoon kosher salt
⅛ teaspoon cayenne pepper (optional)
2 tablespoons olive oil
1 (14- to 16-ounce) package extra-firm tofu, drained and cut into 1-inch pieces

In a small bowl, combine the nutritional yeast, cornstarch, garam masala, salt, cayenne (if using), and olive oil. Stir together to make a paste.

Place the tofu in a lidded container. Add the spice paste mixture and toss to evenly coat the tofu. Label "Masala Marinated Tofu" and store in the fridge.

Cilantro Chutney

Makes about 1½ cups

- 1 cup loosely packed fresh cilantro leaves
- 1 jalapeño chile, seeded and coarsely chopped
- ½ cup plain whole-milk Greek yogurt
- ½ cup raw cashews (whole or pieces)
- 2 garlic cloves, peeled
- ¼ cup fresh lime juice (from about 2 large limes)
- 2 tablespoons avocado oil or other neutral oil
- 1 teaspoon kosher salt
- ¼ teaspoon ground cumin

Combine all the ingredients in a wide-mouth pint jar. Lower an immersion blender into the jar and blend at **HIGH** speed for about 2 minutes, until smooth. (Alternatively, blend all the ingredients in a countertop blender, then transfer to a jar.) Label "Cilantro Chutney" and store in the fridge.

Moroccan-Spiced Meatball Mixture

Serves 4

- 1 pound 93% lean ground turkey
- ½ cup plain breadcrumbs
- 1 large egg
- 2 tablespoons fresh lemon juice
- 2 tablespoons chopped fresh flat-leaf parsley
- 1 teaspoon ras el hanout
- ¾ teaspoon kosher salt

Combine all the ingredients in a large bowl. Use your hands to mix everything together until well combined. Transfer to a tightly lidded container, label "Moroccan-Spiced Meatball Mixture," and store in the fridge.

5.

Supercharged Spaghetti Vegetable Prep

Makes 4 servings

1 medium yellow onion, finely chopped
1 large carrot, peeled and finely chopped
1 red bell pepper, seeded and finely chopped
1 large zucchini, trimmed and finely chopped
2 garlic cloves, minced or pressed

Combine all the vegetables in a zip-top bag or lidded container, label "Supercharged Spaghetti Vegetable Prep," and store in the fridge.

6.

Sausage, Okra, and Pepper Prep

Makes 4 servings

1 medium yellow onion, cut into 1-inch strips
1 red bell pepper, seeded and cut into 1-inch strips
1 (12-ounce) link Polish pork kielbasa, sliced into ½-inch-thick rounds
1 garlic clove, minced or pressed

Combine all the ingredients in a zip-top bag or lidded container, label "Sausage, Okra, and Pepper Prep," and store in the fridge.

Green Bean Prep

Makes 4 servings

8 ounces green beans, trimmed and cut into 1-inch pieces

Put the green beans in a zip-top bag or lidded container, label "Green Bean Prep," and store in the fridge.

Shredded Carrots

Makes 4 servings

3 large carrots, peeled and shredded with a coarse grater

Put the carrots in a zip-top bag or lidded container, label "Shredded Carrots," and store in the fridge.

Meal 1

Supercharged Spaghetti, Cheesy Garlic Toast

Serves 4

- 2 tablespoons olive oil
- Supercharged Spaghetti Vegetable Prep (page 99)
- 1 teaspoon kosher salt
- ¼ teaspoon ground black pepper
- 1 pound 90% lean ground beef
- 8 ounces spaghetti, broken into 3-inch lengths
- 1½ cups low-sodium chicken or vegetable broth
- 1 (14-ounce) can petite diced tomatoes
- ¼ cup tomato paste
- Garlic Toast Spread (page 97)
- 4 thick slices from 1 loaf crusty Italian bread
- Grated parmesan cheese, for serving

Heat the oil in the pressure cooker on the **SAUTÉ** setting for a minute or two. Add the vegetables, salt, and pepper and sauté for 5 minutes, until the vegetables begin to soften. Add the ground beef and sauté, breaking it up with a spatula as it cooks, for about 3 minutes, until no traces of pink remain.

Add the pasta, then pour the broth and diced tomatoes with their juices over the pasta. Add the tomato paste in a dollop on top—do not stir it in. Pressure-cook for 4 minutes at **HIGH** pressure, with a **QUICK** pressure release. Stir to combine everything evenly.

While the pasta is cooking, preheat the air fryer to 400°F. Spread an even layer of the spread on the slices of bread. Add in a single layer directly in the air fryer basket or on the baking sheet of an air fryer oven, lined with parchment paper or aluminum foil, and air-fry for 6 minutes.

Transfer the pasta and garlic bread to plates and serve right away, with parmesan cheese on the side.

Meal 2

Green Bean Rice, Masala Tofu Bites, Cilantro Chutney

Serves 4

1 tablespoon olive oil
½ teaspoon cumin seeds
1 cup basmati rice
1¼ cups low-sodium chicken or vegetable broth
¼ teaspoon kosher salt
Green Bean Prep (page 101)
Masala Marinated Tofu (page 97)
Cilantro Chutney (page 98), for serving

Heat the olive oil and cumin seeds in the pressure cooker on the **SAUTÉ** setting. When the seeds start to bubble a bit and become aromatic, add the rice, broth, and salt and stir to combine. Scatter the green beans over the rice. Pressure-cook on the Rice setting (or for 12 minutes at **LOW** pressure), with a 10-minute **NATURAL** pressure release.

While the rice is cooking, preheat the air fryer to 400°F. Add the marinated tofu in a single layer directly in the air fryer basket or on the baking sheet of an air fryer oven, lined with parchment paper or aluminum foil, and air-fry for 12 minutes.

Transfer the rice and tofu to serving bowls or plates. Serve right away, with the chutney on the side.

Meal 3

Moroccan-Spiced Turkey Meatballs, Carrot Pearl Couscous

Serves 4

- 8 ounces (1¼ cups) pearl or Israeli couscous
- Shredded Carrots (page 101)
- 1½ cups low-sodium chicken or vegetable broth
- 1 tablespoon butter
- Moroccan-Spiced Meatball Mixture (page 98)

Add the couscous, shredded carrots, broth, and butter to the pressure cooker. Stir to combine, then pressure-cook at **HIGH** pressure for 5 minutes, with a **QUICK** pressure release. Stir to evenly mix the carrots in with the couscous.

While the couscous is cooking, preheat the air fryer to 400°F. Use a 1½-tablespoon scoop to portion out meatballs in a single layer directly into the air fryer basket or onto the baking sheet of an air fryer oven, lined with parchment paper or aluminum foil. Air-fry for 10 minutes.

Transfer the meatballs and couscous to serving plates and serve right away.

NOTE: If you've got leftover cilantro chutney from last night's meal, it goes nicely with this one, too.

Meal 4

Sausage, Okra, and Peppers, Buttered Rice

Serves 4

- 1 cup basmati rice
- 1¼ cups low-sodium chicken or vegetable broth
- 1 tablespoon butter
- ½ teaspoon kosher salt, divided
- Sausage, Okra, and Pepper Prep (page 99)
- 1 (12-ounce) frozen cut okra (no need to thaw)
- 1½ tablespoons olive oil
- ¼ teaspoon ground black pepper

Add the rice, broth, butter, and ¼ teaspoon of the salt to the pressure cooker. Pressure-cook on the Rice setting (or for 12 minutes at **LOW** pressure), with a 10-minute **NATURAL** pressure release.

While the rice is cooking, preheat the air fryer to 375°F. Add the prepared sausage and vegetables and the frozen okra in a single layer directly in the air fryer basket or on the baking sheet of an air fryer oven, lined with parchment paper or aluminum foil. Drizzle with the olive oil and sprinkle on the remaining ¼ teaspoon salt and the pepper. Air-fry for 20 minutes, shaking or stirring halfway through cooking.

Transfer the sausages and vegetables and the rice to serving bowls or plates. Serve right away.

Week 7
UMAMI ADVENTURE

Pulling out all the savory stops is a surefire way to make dishes that are craveable, bite after bite. On night one, miso provides a base of umami flavor for the marinated cod, served alongside ramen mixed with edamame and scallions. Tuesday brings an Irish stew–inspired bowl of meatballs and carrots, with cheddar-and-rosemary-studded scones served alongside. Cuban mojo provides the template for citrusy, garlicky marinated pork chops with sides of rice and beans and hearts of palm. A French-style ratatouille includes chickpeas for some vegetarian protein, and parsley-garlic toast is just the tool for swiping your plate clean and enjoying all of the tomatoey sauce.

Week 7 Menu

Miso-Marinated Cod, Edamame and Scallion Ramen

Meatballs and Carrots, Rosemary-Cheddar Scones

Mojo Pork Chops, Rice and Black Beans, Hearts of Palm Salad

Chickpea Ratatouille, Parsley-Garlic Toast

SHOPPING LIST

PRODUCE

- 1 pound carrots
- 2 medium yellow onions
- 1 English cucumber
- 1 cup cherry tomatoes
- 1 medium eggplant
- 1 large zucchini
- 1 red bell pepper
- 1 Roma tomato
- 3 green onions
- 8 garlic cloves
- 1 bunch fresh rosemary
- 1 bunch fresh flat-leaf parsley
- 1 large lime
- ¼ cup orange juice

PANTRY

- 1¼ cups all-purpose flour
- 3 tablespoons granulated sugar
- 2 teaspoons cornstarch
- 1 teaspoon baking powder
- 1 teaspoon toasted sesame seeds
- 1 teaspoon garlic salt
- 1 teaspoon dried oregano
- 1 teaspoon Cuban seasoning (or ½ teaspoon each dried oregano and ground cumin)
- ¼ teaspoon baking soda
- ¼ teaspoon ground cumin
- ⅛ teaspoon ground nutmeg
- 1 (15-ounce) can black beans
- 1 (15-ounce) can chickpeas
- 1 (15-ounce) can hearts of palm
- 3 cups low-sodium chicken or vegetable broth
- ½ cup sake
- ¼ cup white miso paste
- 2 tablespoons coconut oil
- 1 tablespoon soy sauce
- 1 tablespoon tomato paste
- 2 teaspoons red wine vinegar
- 1 teaspoon toasted sesame oil
- 1 teaspoon Dijon mustard
- ½ teaspoon Worcestershire sauce
- 1 cup long-grain white rice
- 3 (3-ounce) packages ramen noodles only (I like Lotus Foods rice ramen.)
- ½ cup panko breadcrumbs
- 1 loaf sourdough bread

DAIRY AND EGGS

- ⅓ cup plain whole-milk Greek yogurt
- ½ cup (2 ounces) shredded cheddar cheese
- ½ cup (1 stick) butter
- 1 large egg

MEAT AND PROTEIN

- 4 (6-ounce) cod fillets
- 1 pound 90% lean ground beef
- 4 (6-ounce) boneless pork loin chops

FROZEN

- 1 (12-ounce) bag shelled edamame (mukimame)

SUNDAY MEAL PREP RECIPES

no cook

pressure cooker

air fryer

oven

stovetop

microwave

Miso-Marinated Cod

Serves 4

4 (6-ounce) cod fillets
½ cup sake
¼ cup white miso paste
3 tablespoons granulated sugar

Place the cod fillets in a lidded container.

In a small bowl, stir together the sake, miso paste, and sugar until thoroughly combined. Spoon the miso mixture evenly over the cod fillets, using your hands to coat them evenly. Label "Miso-Marinated Cod" and store in the fridge.

Meatball Mixture

Serves 4

1 pound 90% lean ground beef
½ cup panko breadcrumbs
1 teaspoon onion powder
1 teaspoon garlic salt
¼ teaspoon ground black pepper
⅛ teaspoon ground nutmeg

Combine all the ingredients in a large bowl. Use your hands to mix everything together until well combined. Transfer to a tightly lidded container, label "Meatball Mixture," and store in the fridge.

3.

Meatball Gravy

Makes about 1 cup

1 cup low-sodium chicken or vegetable broth
1 tablespoon tomato paste
1 teaspoon Dijon mustard
½ teaspoon Worcestershire sauce

Combine all the ingredients in a pint jar. Shake to combine. Label "Meatball Gravy" and store in the fridge.

Rosemary-Cheddar Scones

Makes 4

1¼ cups all-purpose flour
1 teaspoon baking powder
¼ teaspoon baking soda
¼ teaspoon kosher salt
½ cup (2 ounces) shredded cheddar cheese
1 teaspoon chopped fresh rosemary
4 tablespoons cold butter, cut into ⅓-inch cubes
⅓ cup plain whole-milk Greek yogurt
1 large egg

In a large bowl, stir together the flour, baking powder, baking soda, salt, cheese, rosemary, and butter. Use your fingers to smoosh each cube of butter into a thin flake. Add the yogurt and egg and stir until mostly combined. Use your hands to finish mixing, just until a cohesive ball of dough forms.

Transfer the dough to a piece of plastic wrap. Pat the dough into a ½-inch-thick disk, cut the dough into quarters, top it with another piece of plastic wrap, and wrap tightly. Label "Rosemary Cheddar Scones" and store in the fridge.

Mojo Pork Chops

Serves 4

4 (6-ounce) boneless pork loin chops
Juice of 1 large lime
¼ cup orange juice
2 tablespoons olive oil
4 garlic cloves, minced or pressed
1½ teaspoons kosher salt
1 teaspoon dried oregano
¼ teaspoon ground cumin
¼ teaspoon ground black pepper

Place the pork chops in a lidded container or zip-top bag.

In a bowl, whisk together the lime juice, orange juice, olive oil, garlic, salt, oregano, cumin, and black pepper. Pour the mixture over the pork chops, ensuring they are all coated in the marinade. Label "Mojo Pork Chops" and store in the fridge.

Parsley-Garlic Toast Spread

Serves 4 (for 4 slices of toast)

4 tablespoons butter, at room temperature
2 tablespoons chopped fresh flat-leaf parsley
2 garlic cloves, pressed or minced
¼ teaspoon kosher salt

In a small bowl, mix together all the ingredients. Transfer to a piece of plastic wrap, shape into a little log, then wrap tightly. Label "Parsley-Garlic Toast Spread" and store in the fridge.

Hearts of Palm Salad Vinaigrette

Makes about 3 tablespoons

2 tablespoons olive oil
2 teaspoons red wine vinegar
¼ teaspoon kosher salt
A few grinds black pepper

Add all the ingredients to a half-pint jar or other small lidded container. Shake to combine. Label "Hearts of Palm Salad Vinaigrette" and store in the fridge.

Carrot Prep

Makes 4 servings

1 pound carrots, peeled and cut into 1-inch pieces

Put the carrots in a lidded container or zip-top bag, label "Carrot Prep," and store in the fridge.

Hearts of Palm Salad Prep

Makes 4 servings

1 English cucumber, trimmed and cut into ½-inch pieces

¼ medium yellow onion, thinly sliced

2 green onions, thinly sliced

Put all the vegetables in a tightly lidded container or zip-top bag, label "Hearts of Palm Salad Prep," and store in the fridge.

10.

Ratatouille Vegetable Prep

Makes 4 servings

1 medium yellow onion, cut into 1-inch pieces

1 medium eggplant, trimmed and cut into 1-inch pieces

1 large zucchini, trimmed and cut into 1-inch pieces

1 red bell pepper, seeded and cut into 1-inch pieces

1 Roma tomato, chopped

2 garlic cloves, minced or pressed

Put all the vegetables in a tightly lidded container or zip-top bag, label "Ratatouille Vegetable Prep," and store in the fridge.

Meal 1

Miso-Marinated Cod, Edamame and Scallion Ramen

Serves 4

- 1 cup frozen shelled edamame (mukimame)
- 3 (3-ounce) packages ramen (noodles only; discard seasoning packets)
- 1 tablespoon soy sauce
- 1 teaspoon toasted sesame oil
- Miso-Marinated Cod (page 114)
- 1 teaspoon toasted sesame seeds
- 1 green onion

Preheat the air fryer to 375°F.

Heat the edamame according to the package instructions (I microwave mine for 2 minutes in a covered container, with a splash of water).

Cook the ramen noodles according to the package instructions, then drain and toss with the edamame, soy sauce, and sesame oil.

Add the cod in a single layer directly in the air fryer basket or on the baking sheet of an air fryer oven, lined with parchment paper or aluminum foil, and air-fry for 15 minutes.

Transfer the noodles and cod to serving bowls or plates and serve right away, with the sesame seeds sprinkled and green onion snipped over the top.

Meal 2

Meatballs and Carrots, Rosemary-Cheddar Scones

Serves 4

- 1 tablespoon avocado oil or other neutral oil
- Meatball Mixture (page 114)
- Meatball Gravy (page 115)
- Carrots Prep (page 118)
- 2 teaspoons cornstarch
- 2 teaspoons water
- Rosemary-Cheddar Scones (page 115)

Heat the oil in the pressure cooker on the **SAUTÉ** setting for a minute or two. Use a 2½-tablespoon scoop to portion out meatballs straight into the pot. Let the meatballs sear for 3 minutes, then flip them and sear for 2 more minutes.

Add the gravy and carrots, stir gently to combine, then pressure-cook for 10 minutes at **HIGH** pressure, with a **QUICK** pressure release.

Stir together the cornstarch and water, then pour it in with the meatballs and carrots. Return the pressure cooker to the **SAUTÉ** setting for 1 minute, stirring until the gravy is thickened.

While the meatballs and carrots are cooking, preheat the air fryer to 325°F. Place the scones at least 1 inch apart directly in the air fryer basket or on the baking sheet of an air fryer oven, lined with parchment paper or aluminum foil. Air-fry for 12 minutes, until lightly browned and cooked through.

Transfer the meatballs and carrots to serving bowls or plates. Serve right away, with the scones on the side.

Meal 3

Mojo Pork Chops, Rice and Black Beans, Hearts of Palm Salad

Serves 4

2 tablespoons coconut oil
1 teaspoon Cuban seasoning (or ½ teaspoon each dried oregano and ground cumin)
½ teaspoon kosher salt
1 cup long-grain white rice
1 (15-ounce) can black beans, drained and rinsed
1½ cups low-sodium chicken or vegetable broth
Mojo Pork Chops (page 116)
Hearts of Palm Salad Prep (page 119)
1 (15-ounce) can hearts of palm, drained and cut into ½-inch slices
1 cup cherry tomatoes
Hearts of Palm Salad Vinaigrette (page 118)

Heat the coconut oil in the pressure cooker on the **SAUTÉ** setting for a minute or two. Add the Cuban seasoning blend and let it bubble and become aromatic for just a few seconds, then add the salt, rice, beans, and broth. Stir to combine, then pressure-cook on the Rice setting (or at **LOW** pressure for 12 minutes), with a 10-minute pressure release.

While the rice and beans are cooking, preheat the air fryer to 375°F. Add the pork chops in a single layer directly in the air fryer basket or on the baking sheet of an air fryer oven, lined with parchment paper or aluminum foil, and air-fry for 20 minutes.

In a bowl, toss the hearts of palm salad prep ingredients with the hearts of palm, tomatoes, and vinaigrette.

Transfer the rice and beans, pork chops, and salad to serving plates and serve right away.

Meal 4

Chickpea Ratatouille, Parsley-Garlic Toast

Serves 4

2 tablespoons olive oil
Ratatouille Vegetable Prep (page 119)
½ teaspoon kosher salt
½ teaspoon Italian seasoning
½ cup low-sodium vegetable or chicken broth
1 (15-ounce) can chickpeas, drained and rinsed
4 thick slices from 1 loaf sourdough bread
Parsley-Garlic Toast Spread (page 116), room temperature

Add the olive oil, ratatouille vegetable mixture, salt, Italian seasoning, broth, and chickpeas to the pressure cooker and stir to combine. Pressure-cook for 2 minutes at **LOW** pressure, with a **QUICK** pressure release.

While the ratatouille is cooking, preheat the air fryer to 400°F. Spread the slices of bread evenly with the parsley-garlic toast spread. Add in a single layer directly in the air fryer basket or on the baking sheet of an air fryer oven, lined with parchment paper or aluminum foil, and air-fry for 6 minutes.

Transfer the ratatouille to serving bowls and serve right away, with the toast on the side.

Week 8

SUMMER SIZZLERS

Whether it's summertime or you just need a week of sunny flavors, turn to this menu. Chicken cutlets are seasoned ahead of time so they're ready to be air-fried and served with a Caprese-inspired pasta salad. Lime crema adds summery flavor to Tuesday's shrimp tostadas, and you can spoon some on top of the black bean and corn salad, too. Tomatoes and zucchini bring their garden freshness to Wednesday's vegetarian meal, an elevated take on tomato soup and grilled cheese. For Thursday, boneless chicken thighs are baked in a sticky-sweet glaze and served with a salad that includes sweet nectarines, crisp lettuce, and hearty wheat berries.

Week 8 Menu

Dry-Brined Chicken Cutlets, Pasta with Tomatoes and Mozzarella Pearls

Smoky Shrimp Tostadas, Black Bean and Corn Salad, Lime Crema

Tomato and White Bean Soup, Zucchini Toast

Apricot-Dijon Chicken Thighs, Nectarine Chopped Salad

SHOPPING LIST

PRODUCE

- 1½ pounds zucchini
- 2 romaine lettuce hearts
- 1 medium yellow onion
- 3 carrots
- 3 celery stalks
- 2 green onions
- 2 Roma tomatoes
- 2 garlic cloves
- 1 bunch fresh basil
- 1 bunch fresh cilantro
- 2 nectarines
- 1 large lemon
- 2 large limes

PANTRY

- 1 teaspoon brown sugar
- ½ teaspoon smoked paprika
- ¼ teaspoon red pepper flakes
- ¼ teaspoon paprika
- 1 (15-ounce) can black beans
- 1 (15-ounce) can white beans
- 1 (14-ounce) can petite diced tomatoes
- 1 (8-ounce) jar apricot jam
- ¼ cup plus 1 tablespoon Dijon mustard
- 2 tablespoons mayonnaise
- 2 tablespoons balsamic vinegar
- 1 tablespoon red wine vinegar
- 1½ cups low-sodium chicken or vegetable broth
- 8 ounces penne pasta
- 8 corn tostadas (I like Guerrero brand.)
- 1 cup wheat berries
- 1 loaf French bread

DAIRY

- ½ cup sour cream
- 8 ounces mozzarella cheese pearls

MEAT AND PROTEIN

- 1½ pounds chicken breast cutlets
- 1½ pounds boneless, skinless chicken thighs

FROZEN

- 1 pound frozen peeled and deveined jumbo shrimp
- 1½ cups frozen corn

SUNDAY MEAL PREP RECIPES

no cook

pressure cooker

air fryer

oven

stovetop

microwave

1.

Dry-Brined Chicken Cutlets

Serves 4

1 teaspoon Italian seasoning
1 teaspoon garlic powder
1 teaspoon kosher salt
1 teaspoon brown sugar
¼ teaspoon red pepper flakes
¼ teaspoon paprika
1½ pounds chicken breast cutlets

In a small bowl, mix the Italian seasoning, garlic powder, salt, sugar, red pepper flakes, and paprika. Sprinkle the mixture evenly over the chicken breast cutlets, covering both sides. Transfer to a lidded container or zip-top bag, label "Dry-Brined Chicken Cutlets," and store in the fridge.

2.

Apricot-Dijon Chicken Thighs

Serves 4

1½ pounds boneless, skinless chicken thighs
¼ cup Dijon mustard
¼ cup apricot jam
1 tablespoon avocado oil or other neutral oil
½ teaspoon garlic powder
½ teaspoon kosher salt
¼ teaspoon ground black pepper

Add the chicken thighs to a lidded container or zip-top bag.

In a bowl, mix up the mustard, jam, oil, garlic powder, salt, and pepper. Pour the mixture over the chicken thighs, tossing to coat them evenly. Label "Apricot-Dijon Chicken Thighs" and store in the fridge.

3.

Lemony Vinaigrette

Makes about ⅔ cup

¼ cup olive oil or other neutral oil
3 tablespoons fresh lemon juice
1 tablespoon red wine vinegar
1 tablespoon apricot jam
1 tablespoon Dijon mustard
¼ teaspoon garlic powder
½ teaspoon kosher salt
¼ teaspoon ground black pepper

Add all the ingredients to a half-pint jar or other small lidded container. Shake to combine. Label "Lemony Vinaigrette" and store in the fridge.

4.

Balsamic Vinaigrette

Makes about ¼ cup

2 tablespoons balsamic vinegar
2 tablespoons olive oil
½ teaspoon kosher salt
⅛ teaspoon ground black pepper

Add all the ingredients to a half-pint jar or other small lidded container. Shake to combine. Label "Balsamic Vinaigrette" and store in the fridge.

Shrimp Marinade/ Vinaigrette

Makes about ½ cup

⅓ cup olive oil
Grated zest of ½ lime
2 tablespoons fresh lime juice
1 teaspoon kosher salt
1 teaspoon chili powder
½ teaspoon smoked paprika

Add all the ingredients to a half-pint jar or other small lidded container. Shake to combine. Label "Shrimp Marinade/Vinaigrette" and store in the fridge.

Lime Crema

Makes about ¾ cup

½ cup sour cream
2 tablespoons mayonnaise
Grated zest of ½ lime
2 tablespoons fresh lime juice
½ teaspoon kosher salt

Add all the ingredients to a half-pint jar or other small lidded container. Stir to combine. Label "Lime Crema" and store in the fridge.

7.

Pasta Salad Vegetable Prep

Makes 4 servings

2 Roma tomatoes, diced
4 fresh basil sprigs

Put the tomatoes and basil in a lidded container or zip-top bag. Label "Pasta Salad Vegetable Prep" and store in the fridge.

8.

Nectarine and Lettuce Prep

Makes 4 servings

2 nectarines, pitted and diced
2 romaine lettuce hearts, chopped into 1-inch pieces

Put the nectarines and lettuce in a lidded container or zip-top bag, label "Nectarine and Lettuce Prep," and store in the fridge.

Green Onion and Cilantro Prep

Makes 4 servings

2 green onions, sliced
½ cup fresh cilantro leaves, chopped

Transfer the green onions and the cilantro to a lidded container or zip-top bag, label "Green Onion and Cilantro Prep," and store in the fridge.

Tomato and White Bean Soup Prep

Makes 4 servings

2 garlic cloves, chopped
1 medium yellow onion, chopped
3 celery stalks, chopped
3 carrots, peeled and diced

Put all the vegetables in a lidded container or zip-top bag, label "Vegetables for Tomato and White Bean Soup," and store in the fridge.

Zucchini Confit

Makes 4 servings

1 teaspoon kosher salt

1½ pounds zucchini, trimmed and shredded

¼ cup olive oil

In a large bowl, sprinkle the salt over the zucchini, then toss to combine. Let sit for 15 minutes. Use your hands to wring out the zucchini a bit. Discard the liquid that settles in the bowl.

Heat the olive oil in the pressure cooker on the **SAUTÉ** setting for a minute or two. Add the zucchini and sauté for about 20 minutes, until the zucchini has softened, cooked down considerably in volume, and just begun to brown on the bottom of the pot. Turn off the pressure cooker and let the zucchini sit for 1 minute, then use a wooden spoon to nudge up any browned bits from the bottom of the pot and stir them in. Transfer to a container and let cool to room temperature. Label "Zucchini Confit" and store in the fridge.

Cooked Penne Pasta

Serves 4

8 ounces penne pasta

½ teaspoon kosher salt

Add the pasta, salt, and 2 cups water to the pressure cooker. Pressure-cook for 5 minutes at **HIGH** pressure, with a **QUICK** pressure release. Drain any excess liquid in a colander, then transfer the pasta to a lidded container and let cool to room temperature. Label "Cooked Penne Pasta" and store in the fridge.

13.

Steamed Wheat Berries

Serves 4

1 cup wheat berries
½ teaspoon kosher salt
1¼ cups water

Add the wheat berries, salt, and 1¼ cups water to the pressure cooker. Pressure-cook for 30 minutes at **HIGH** pressure, with a 10-minute **NATURAL** pressure release. Drain any excess liquid in a colander, then transfer the wheat berries to a lidded container and let cool to room temperature. Label "Steamed Wheat Berries" and store in the fridge.

Meal 1

Dry-Brined Chicken Cutlets, Pasta with Tomatoes and Mozzarella Pearls

Serves 4

Dry-Brined Chicken Cutlets (page 131)

1 tablespoon avocado oil or other neutral oil

Cooked Penne Pasta (page 136)

Pasta Salad Vegetable Prep (page 134)

8 ounces mozzarella cheese pearls

Balsamic Vinaigrette (page 132)

4 fresh basil sprigs

Preheat the air fryer to 400°F. Add the chicken cutlets in a single layer directly in the air fryer basket or on the baking sheet of an air fryer oven, lined with parchment paper or aluminum foil. Drizzle them with the avocado oil. Air-fry for 10 minutes.

While the chicken is cooking, assemble the pasta salad: Combine the pasta, vegetables, cheese, and vinaigrette in a salad bowl. Add the basil, discarding the stems and ripping the leaves as you add them. Toss to combine.

Transfer the chicken cutlets and pasta salad to serving plates or bowls. Serve right away.

Meal 2

Smoky Shrimp Tostadas, Black Bean and Corn Salad, Lime Crema

Serves 4

- 1 pound frozen jumbo peeled and deveined shrimp, thawed according to package instructions
- Shrimp Marinade/Vinaigrette (page 133)
- 1 (15-ounce) can black beans, drained and rinsed
- 1½ cups frozen corn, thawed according to package instructions
- Green Onion and Cilantro Prep (page 135)
- 8 corn tostadas (such as Guerrero)
- Lime Crema (page 133)

In a bowl, toss the shrimp with half of the vinaigrette. Set aside to marinate for 10 minutes.

While the shrimp is marinating, in another bowl, toss the black beans, corn, and the green onions and cilantro with the remaining vinaigrette.

Preheat the air fryer to 400°F. Add the shrimp in a single layer directly in the air fryer basket or on the baking sheet of an air fryer oven, lined with parchment paper or aluminum foil, and air-fry for 4 minutes.

Place 2 tostadas on each serving plate. Scoop the bean and corn salad onto the tostadas, then top with the shrimp and drizzle with the crema. Serve right away.

NOTE: If serving small children, you can substitute warmed corn tortillas for the tostadas.

Meal 3

Tomato and White Bean Soup, Zucchini Toast

Serves 4

- 2 tablespoons olive oil
- Vegetables for Tomato and White Bean Soup (page 135)
- ½ teaspoon Italian seasoning
- 1½ cups low-sodium chicken or vegetable broth
- 1 (15-ounce) can white beans, drained and rinsed
- 1 (14-ounce) can petite diced tomatoes
- Zucchini Confit (page 136)
- 4 (1½-inch-thick) slices French bread

Heat the olive oil in the pressure cooker on the **SAUTÉ** setting for a minute or two. Add the vegetables and Italian seasoning and sauté for 5 minutes, until the onion is beginning to soften. Add the broth, white beans, and tomatoes with their juices, then pressure-cook at **HIGH** pressure for 3 minutes, with a 5-minute **NATURAL** pressure release.

While the soup is cooking, preheat the air fryer to 400°F. Spread ¼ cup of the zucchini confit onto each slice of bread. Add the toasts in a single layer directly in the air fryer basket or on the baking sheet of an air fryer oven, lined with parchment paper or aluminum foil, and air-fry for 6 minutes.

Ladle the soup into serving bowls and serve right away, with the zucchini toast on the side.

NOTE: If you prefer a smooth texture to your soup, blend it with an immersion blender (or in a countertop blender) after cooking.

Meal 4

Apricot-Dijon Chicken Thighs, Nectarine Chopped Salad

Serves 4

Apricot-Dijon Chicken Thighs (page 131)
Nectarine and Lettuce Prep (page 134)
Steamed Wheat Berries (page 137)
Lemony Vinaigrette (page 132)

Preheat the air fryer to 375°F. Add the chicken thighs in a single layer directly in the air fryer basket or on the baking sheet of an air fryer oven, lined with parchment paper or aluminum foil, and air-fry for 18 minutes.

While the chicken is cooking, assemble the salad: Add the nectarines, lettuce, wheat berries, and vinaigrette to a salad bowl and toss to combine.

Transfer the chicken and salad to serving bowls or plates and serve right away.

Week 9

AUTUMN HARVEST

Fall into a menu of autumn flavors this week. Roast up an early fall harvest of eggplants and bell peppers, blend them into a Balkan-inspired spread, then add a generous amount to flatbread wraps with smoky pork sausages tucked inside. Next, bake up a dish of tomatoey lima beans topped with melty cheese and serve with crusty bread, and you've got the flavors of pizza in a protein- and fiber-packed vegetarian skillet. Wednesday, have a meatloaf made with a roster of classic fall ingredients: turkey, apples, and sage. Mashed cauliflower, made extra flavorful with cheddar cheese, is served alongside. For the last of the week's meals, air-fry some pork chops in a mustard and brown sugar marinade and serve them with a pile of buttery, garlicky green beans.

Week 9 Menu

Sausage Wraps with Eggplant and Bell Pepper Spread and Garlic Sauce

Pizza-Style Lima Beans

Apple and Sage Turkey Meatloaf, Cheesy Mashed Cauliflower

Mustard and Brown Sugar Pork Chops, Garlic Butter Green Beans

SHOPPING LIST

PRODUCE

- 1 large red bell pepper
- 1 medium eggplant
- 1 large head cauliflower
- 1 medium yellow onion
- 1 pound green beans
- 2 heads garlic
- 1 bunch fresh sage
- 1 lemon
- 1 medium apple

PANTRY

- ¼ cup brown sugar
- 1 teaspoon garlic salt
- ¼ teaspoon red pepper flakes
- ¼ teaspoon dried oregano
- 1 (12- to 14-ounce) jar pizza sauce (Rao's and Carbone are my favorites.)
- 6 tablespoons ketchup
- ¼ cup Dijon mustard
- 2 tablespoons apple cider vinegar
- 1 tablespoon red wine vinegar
- ½ cup panko breadcrumbs
- 1 loaf French bread
- 8 dinner rolls (or use homemade)
- 4 flatbread wraps or pitas

DAIRY AND EGGS

- ¼ cup sour cream
- 1 cup (4 ounces) shredded sharp cheddar cheese
- 2 cups (8 ounces) shredded mozzarella cheese
- 3½ tablespoons butter
- 1 large egg

MEAT AND PROTEIN

- 1 pound 93% lean ground turkey
- 4 (6-ounce) boneless pork chops
- 4 (4-ounce) smoked pork sausages

FROZEN

- 2 (12-ounce) bags frozen baby lima beans

SUNDAY MEAL PREP RECIPES

no cook

pressure cooker

air fryer

oven

stovetop

microwave

Garlic Sauce

Makes about 1½ cups

- 1 head garlic, cloves peeled
- ¾ cup avocado oil or other neutral oil
- 1 tablespoon fresh lemon juice
- 1 teaspoon kosher salt

Combine all the ingredients in a wide-mouth pint jar. Lower an immersion blender all the way to the bottom of the jar. In half-second pulses, blend the mixture into an emulsified sauce, slowly bringing the immersion blender back up through the ingredients as you go. By the time you get to the top, you'll have a fully blended jar of garlic sauce. (Alternatively, blend all the ingredients in a countertop blender, then transfer to a jar.) Label "Garlic Sauce" and store in the fridge.

Apple and Sage Turkey Meatloaf Mixture

Serves 4 to 6

- 1 pound 93% lean ground turkey
- 1 medium apple, peeled, cored, and shredded with a coarse grater
- ½ cup finely chopped yellow onion
- 2 garlic cloves, minced or pressed
- 1 tablespoon fresh chopped sage
- 1 large egg
- ½ cup panko breadcrumbs
- 1 teaspoon kosher salt
- ¼ teaspoon ground black pepper

In a large bowl, combine all the ingredients. Mix with your hands until fully combined. Transfer to a lidded container, label "Apple and Sage Turkey Meatloaf Mixture," and store in the fridge.

Cheesy Cauliflower Prep

Serves 4

1 large head cauliflower, cut into florets
1 cup (4 ounces) shredded sharp cheddar cheese
2 tablespoons butter
¼ cup sour cream
½ teaspoon garlic salt
¼ teaspoon ground black pepper

Put the cauliflower in a zip-top bag or lidded container, label "Cauliflower Prep," and store in the fridge.

Add the shredded cheddar, butter, sour cream, garlic salt, and pepper to a pint jar or other lidded container, label "Cheesy Sauce Ingredients," and store in the fridge.

Green Bean Prep

Makes 4 servings

1 pound green beans, trimmed

Put the green beans in a zip-top bag or lidded container, label "Green Bean Prep," and store in the fridge.

5.

Eggplant and Bell Pepper Spread

Makes about 1¼ cups

- 1 large red bell pepper, seeded and cut into 1-inch pieces
- 1 medium eggplant, peeled and cut into 1-inch pieces
- 3 tablespoons olive oil, divided
- ¾ teaspoon kosher salt
- 1 tablespoon red wine vinegar
- 1 large garlic clove, pressed or minced

Preheat the air fryer to 400°F. In a bowl, toss the bell pepper and eggplant with 1 tablespoon of the olive oil and the salt. Add the vegetables in a single layer directly in the air fryer basket or on the baking sheet of an air fryer oven, lined with parchment paper or aluminum foil, and air-fry for 15 minutes.

Transfer the vegetables to a food processor, along with the remaining 2 tablespoons olive oil, vinegar, and garlic. Process in pulses until the spread is at your desired level of chunkiness—I like to leave it a bit coarse, with visible pieces of pepper and eggplant, which takes about a dozen 1-second pulses. Scrape down the sides of the processor between pulses, if needed.

Transfer the spread to a pint jar or other lidded container, label "Eggplant and Bell Pepper Spread," and store in the fridge.

6.

Mustard and Brown Sugar Pork Chops

Serves 4

- 4 (6-ounce) boneless pork chops
- ¼ cup Dijon mustard
- ¼ cup brown sugar
- 2 tablespoons apple cider vinegar
- 2 tablespoons avocado oil or other neutral oil
- 2 garlic cloves, minced or pressed
- 1 teaspoon kosher salt
- ½ teaspoon ground black pepper

Add the pork chops to a lidded container or zip-top bag.

In a bowl, stir together the mustard, brown sugar, vinegar, oil, garlic, salt, and pepper. Pour over the pork chops and toss to combine, making sure they are completely coated in the marinade. Label "Mustard and Brown Sugar Pork Chops" and store in the fridge.

Meal 1

Sausage Wraps with Eggplant and Bell Pepper Spread and Garlic Sauce

Serves 4

- 4 (4-ounce) smoked pork sausages
- 4 flatbread wraps or pitas
- Eggplant and Bell Pepper Spread (page 151)
- Garlic Sauce (page 149)

Preheat the air fryer to 400°F. Add the sausages in a single layer directly in the air fryer basket or on the baking sheet of an air fryer oven, lined with parchment paper or aluminum foil, and air-fry for 10 minutes. During the last 2 minutes of cooking, place the pitas right on top of the sausages in the air fryer, to allow them to warm through.

Spread the eggplant and bell pepper spread and garlic sauce on the warmed pitas and transfer them to serving plates, then add the sausages on top. Serve right away.

Meal 2

Pizza-Style Lima Beans

Serves 4 to 6

- 2 (12-ounce) bags frozen baby lima beans, thawed according to package instructions
- 1 (12- to 14-ounce) jar pizza sauce
- 3 tablespoons olive oil
- 2 cups (8 ounces) shredded mozzarella cheese
- ¼ teaspoon red pepper flakes
- ¼ teaspoon dried oregano
- 1 loaf French bread, cut into thick slices

Preheat the air fryer oven or regular oven to 350°F. In an 8-inch square baking dish, stir together the lima beans, pizza sauce, and olive oil. Sprinkle the mozzarella cheese, red pepper flakes, and oregano evenly over the beans. Bake for about 25 minutes, until the cheese is bubbling and beginning to brown in spots.

Spoon the beans onto serving plates or into bowls and serve right away, with French bread on the side.

NOTE: You can also add your favorite pizza toppings on top of the cheese. Mini pepperoni slices, sliced olives, sliced onions, green bell peppers, and crumbled cooked Italian sausage are some of my family's favorites.

Meal 3

Apple and Sage Turkey Meatloaf, Cheesy Mashed Cauliflower

Serves 4 to 6

- Apple and Sage Turkey Meatloaf Mixture (page 149)
- 6 tablespoons ketchup
- Cauliflower Prep (page 150)
- Cheesy Sauce Ingredients (page 150)

Preheat the air fryer to 375°F. Form the meatloaf mixture into 6 (½-cup) loaves, about 1 inch thick. Add the meatloaves to the air fryer in a single layer directly in the air fryer basket or on the baking sheet of an air fryer oven, lined with parchment paper or aluminum foil, and air-fry for 20 minutes, or until the loaves are well browned and measure 165°F in the center when measured with an instant-read thermometer. Top each meatloaf with 1 tablespoon ketchup.

While the meatloaf is cooking, pour a cup of water into the pressure cooker. Add the cauliflower to a steamer basket and place it in the pot. Pressure-cook for 3 minutes at high pressure, with a quick pressure release. Remove the steamer basket from the pot, pour out the water, then return the cauliflower to the pot. Add the cheesy sauce ingredients and use a potato masher or immersion blender to mash the cauliflower until smooth.

Transfer the meatloaves and cauliflower to serving plates. Serve right away.

Meal 4

Mustard and Brown Sugar Pork Chops, Garlic Butter Green Beans

Serves 4

- Mustard and Brown Sugar Pork Chops (page 151)
- Green Bean Prep (page 150)
- 1½ tablespoons butter
- ½ teaspoon garlic salt
- 8 dinner rolls, store-bought or homemade (page 206)

Preheat the air fryer to 375°F. Add the pork chops in a single layer directly in the air fryer basket or on the baking sheet of an air fryer oven, lined with parchment paper or aluminum foil, and air-fry for 20 minutes.

While the pork chops are cooking, pour a cup of water into the pressure cooker. Add the green beans to a steamer basket and place it in the pot. Pressure-cook for 2 minutes at **HIGH** pressure, with a **QUICK** pressure release. Remove the steamer basket from the pot, pour out the water, then return the green beans to the pot. Add the butter and garlic salt and toss to combine.

Transfer the pork chops, green beans, and dinner rolls to serving plates. Serve right away.

Week 10
CULINARY PASSPORT

Let your pantry take you on a journey to France, Greece, Korea, and North Africa this week. These aren't authentic meals by any stretch, but the variety in ingredients and flavor profiles will make you feel like your taste buds have traveled all over the globe. Rosemary and Dijon are a classic pairing in French cuisine, and here they create a flavorful paste for topping salmon. A hearty sweet potato and lentil salad rounds out the meal. Next, the flavors of gyros are made weeknight-friendly in the form of a smash pita. The spiced ground beef cooks right on the bread, and a diced Greek salad makes a fresh and crunchy topping. Day three puts Korean flavors into a Mexican template, with bulgogi-filled quesadillas and a kimchi-spiked guacamole. Last, a North African–inspired combo of lemon and coriander makes for flavorful chicken thighs, and it's paired with a honey butter–topped side of butternut squash.

Week 10 Menu

Rosemary-Dijon Salmon, Roasted Sweet Potato and Lentil Salad

Gyro Smash Pitas, Diced Greek Salad

Bulgogi Quesadillas, Kimchi Guacamole

Lemon-Coriander Chicken, Butternut Squash with Honey Butter

SHOPPING LIST

PRODUCE

- 1 (2-pound) butternut squash
- 1 pound sweet potatoes
- 2 Roma tomatoes
- ½ English cucumber
- 1 large red bell pepper
- 1 medium yellow onion
- 5 garlic cloves
- 4 cups baby arugula
- 1 bunch fresh rosemary
- 1 bunch fresh flat-leaf parsley
- 1 large avocado
- 1 large lemon

PANTRY

- 2 teaspoons ground coriander
- ¼ teaspoon ground cinnamon
- ¼ teaspoon dried oregano
- ¼ cup kimchi
- ¼ cup pitted kalamata olives
- 2 tablespoons plus 2 teaspoons red wine vinegar
- 2 tablespoons honey
- 2 tablespoons soy sauce
- 2 tablespoons gochujang
- 1 tablespoon plus 1 teaspoon Dijon mustard
- ½ teaspoon garlic salt
- 1½ teaspoons toasted sesame oil
- 1 cup green lentils or French lentils (lentilles du Puy)
- 4 pitas
- 8 fajita-size flour tortillas

DAIRY

- 4 ounces cream cheese
- ¼ cup plain whole-milk Greek yogurt
- 2 cups (8 ounces) shredded mozzarella cheese
- ¾ cup (4 ounces) crumbled feta cheese
- 2 tablespoons butter

MEAT AND PROTEIN

- 2 pounds 90% lean ground beef
- 2 pounds bone-in, skin-on chicken thighs
- 4 (6-ounce) salmon fillets

SUNDAY MEAL PREP RECIPES

no cook

pressure cooker

air fryer

oven

stovetop

microwave

Rosemary-Dijon Mixture

Makes about ¼ cup (for 1½ pounds of salmon)

- 1 tablespoon Dijon mustard
- 1 tablespoon honey
- 1 tablespoon olive oil
- 3 garlic cloves, minced or pressed
- 1½ teaspoons fresh chopped rosemary
- ½ teaspoon kosher salt
- ¼ teaspoon ground black pepper

Add all the ingredients to a small jar or other lidded container. Stir to combine. Label "Rosemary-Dijon Mixture" and store in the fridge.

Gyro Meat Mixture

Serves 4

- 1½ teaspoons Italian seasoning
- 1 teaspoon ground coriander
- 1 teaspoon garlic powder
- 1 teaspoon kosher salt
- ¼ teaspoon ground cinnamon
- ¼ teaspoon ground black pepper
- 1 pound 90% lean ground beef

In a large bowl, stir together the Italian seasoning, coriander, garlic powder, salt, cinnamon, and pepper until evenly combined. Add the ground beef and use your hands to knead the spices into the meat until they're evenly distributed. Transfer to a tightly lidded container or zip-top bag, label "Gyro Meat Mixture," and store in the fridge.

Bulgogi Beef Mixture

Serves 4

2 tablespoons soy sauce
2 tablespoons gochujang
1½ teaspoons toasted sesame oil
2 garlic cloves, minced
1 pound 90% lean ground beef

In a large bowl, stir together the soy sauce, gochujang, sesame oil, and garlic. Add the ground beef and use your hands to knead until the mixture is evenly combined. Transfer to a tightly lidded container or zip-top bag, label "Bulgogi Beef Mixture," and store in the fridge.

Lemon-Coriander Chicken

Serves 4

1¼ teaspoons kosher salt
1 teaspoon ground coriander
1 teaspoon garlic powder
½ teaspoon ground black pepper
Grated zest and juice of 1 large lemon
2 tablespoons olive oil
2 pounds bone-in, skin-on chicken thighs

Stir together the salt, coriander, garlic powder, black pepper, lemon zest, lemon juice, and olive oil in a lidded container or a gallon zip-top bag draped over a cup or jar. Add the chicken and toss it in the marinade until all of the thighs are evenly coated. Label "Lemon-Coriander Chicken" and store in the fridge.

5.

Greek Salad Vegetables

- 2 Roma tomatoes, diced
- ½ English cucumber, diced
- 1 large red bell pepper, seeded and diced
- ¼ medium yellow onion, diced
- ¼ cup pitted kalamata olives, roughly chopped

Put all the ingredients in a tightly lidded container or zip-top bag, label "Greek Salad Vegetables," and store in the fridge.

6.

Greek Salad Vinaigrette

Makes about 2 tablespoons

- 1 tablespoon olive oil
- 2 teaspoons red wine vinegar
- ¼ teaspoon dried oregano
- ¼ teaspoon kosher salt

Add all the ingredients to a small jar or other lidded container, label "Greek Salad Vinaigrette," and store in the fridge.

Whipped Feta

Makes about 1½ cups

¾ cup (4 ounces) crumbled feta cheese
4 ounces cream cheese, at room temperature
¼ cup plain whole-milk Greek yogurt
2 tablespoons olive oil

Combine all the ingredients in a wide-mouth pint jar. Lower an immersion blender into the jar and blend until whipped and smooth, about 1 minute. (Alternatively, blend all the ingredients in a countertop blender, then transfer to a jar.) Label "Whipped Feta" and store in the fridge.

Lentil Salad Vinaigrette

Makes about ½ cup

¼ cup olive oil
2 tablespoons red wine vinegar
1 tablespoon chopped fresh flat-leaf parsley
1 teaspoon Dijon mustard
½ teaspoon garlic salt

Add all the ingredients to a small jar or other lidded container. Shake to combine. Label "Lentil Salad Vinaigrette" and store in the fridge.

Butternut Squash Prep

Serves 4

1 (2-pound) butternut squash

Peel the squash, cut it into quarters, and scoop out the seeds. Cut the peeled squash into 1-inch pieces. Transfer to a zip-top bag or lidded container, label “Butternut Squash Prep,” and store in the fridge.

Cooked Lentils

Makes about 2½ cups

1 cup green lentils or French lentils (lentilles du Puy)

1 teaspoon kosher salt

Pour a cup of water into the pressure cooker. Place a raised wire steam rack in the pot, and place a 1½-quart stainless-steel bowl on the rack. Add the lentils, salt, and 1½ cups water to the bowl. Pressure-cook at **HIGH** pressure for 7 minutes for French lentils or 10 minutes for regular green lentils, with a 10-minute **NATURAL** pressure release.

Transfer the lentils to a sheet pan and spread them out in an even layer to cool to room temperature, about 20 minutes. Transfer to a lidded container or zip-top bag, label “Cooked Lentils,” and store in the fridge.

11.

 Roasted Sweet Potatoes

Makes 4 servings (mixed into salad)

1 pound sweet potatoes, peeled and cut into ½-inch cubes

1 tablespoon avocado oil or other neutral oil

¼ teaspoon kosher salt

Preheat the air fryer to 375°F. Put the sweet potatoes in a bowl and toss them with the oil and salt. Add the sweet potatoes in a single layer directly in the air fryer basket or on the baking sheet of an air fryer oven, lined with parchment paper or aluminum foil, and air-fry for 10 minutes.

Let the sweet potatoes cool to room temperature. Transfer them to a lidded container or zip-top bag, label "Roasted Sweet Potatoes," and store in the fridge.

Meal 1

Rosemary-Dijon Salmon, Roasted Sweet Potato and Lentil Salad

Serves 4

- Rosemary-Dijon Mixture (page 163)
- 4 (6-ounce) salmon fillets
- Roasted Sweet Potatoes (page 169)
- Cooked Lentils (page 168)
- Lentil Salad Vinaigrette (page 166)
- 4 cups baby arugula

Preheat the air fryer to 400°F. Spread the rosemary-Dijon mixture onto the salmon fillets, about 1 tablespoon per fillet. Add the salmon in a single layer directly in the air fryer basket or on the baking sheet of an air fryer oven, lined with parchment paper or aluminum foil, and air-fry for 10 minutes.

While the salmon is cooking, add the sweet potatoes, lentils, vinaigrette, and arugula to a salad bowl and toss to combine.

Transfer the salmon and salad to serving plates and serve right away.

Meal 2

Gyro Smash Pitas, Diced Greek Salad

Serves 4

- Gyro Meat Mixture (page 163)
- 4 pitas
- Greek Salad Vegetables (page 165)
- Greek Salad Vinaigrette (page 165)
- Whipped Feta (page 166)

Divide the gyro meat mixture evenly into 4 portions. Spread out each portion on a pita in a thin layer, all the way to the edge of the pita.

Preheat a large nonstick skillet or griddle on the stove over medium heat. Add as many pitas as will fit, meat side down, and let cook for 4 minutes without moving. Flip the pitas, then let them cook for 1 more minute on the bread side.

While the pitas are cooking, in a salad bowl, toss the Greek salad vegetables with the vinaigrette.

Transfer the pitas to serving plates. Add the salad on top of the pitas along with a dollop of whipped feta. Serve right away.

Meal 3

Bulgogi Quesadillas, Kimchi Guacamole

Serves 4

- 8 fajita-size flour tortillas
- Avocado oil spray
- 2 cups (8 ounces) shredded mozzarella cheese
- Bulgogi Beef Mixture (page 164)
- 1 large avocado, peeled and pitted
- ¼ cup kimchi, coarsely chopped

Preheat a conventional oven to 425°F. Place 4 of the tortillas on a sheet pan, spray them lightly with avocado oil, flip them over, and sprinkle ¼ cup mozzarella onto each tortilla. Set aside.

Heat a large skillet on the stove over medium heat. Add the beef mixture and sauté for about 10 minutes, or until any liquid has evaporated and the beef is cooked through and beginning to brown. Spoon the cooked beef onto the tortillas, sprinkle the remaining cheese on top, add the second tortillas, then spray them lightly with the avocado oil.

Bake the quesadillas for 15 minutes, flipping halfway through the cooking time.

While the quesadillas are cooking, in a bowl, use a fork to mash the avocado with the kimchi.

Transfer the quesadillas to serving plates, cut them into wedges, and serve right away, with the kimchi guac on the side.

NOTE: Alternatively, you can air-fry the quesadillas one at a time at 375°F, or cook them in a skillet on the stove over medium heat for 6 minutes, flipping halfway through. If you need to make only one or two quesadillas at mealtime (for instance, if not all your family is having dinner at the same time), then air-frying or cooking on the stove is the way to go! In this case, you can sauté the beef mixture in the pressure cooker on the **SAUTÉ** setting, then leave it on Keep Warm so everyone can make their quesadillas with the hot ground beef when they're ready.

Meal 4

Lemon-Coriander Chicken, Butternut Squash with Honey Butter

Serves 4

- Lemon-Coriander Chicken (page 164)
- Butternut Squash Prep (page 168)
- 2 tablespoons butter
- 1 tablespoon honey
- ½ teaspoon kosher salt

Preheat the air fryer to 375°F. Add the chicken thighs in a single layer directly in the air fryer basket or on the baking sheet of an air fryer oven, lined with parchment paper or aluminum foil, and air-fry for 25 minutes.

While the chicken thighs are cooking, pour a cup of water into the pressure cooker, add the squash to a steamer basket, and place it in the pot. Pressure-cook for 3 minutes at high pressure, with a quick pressure release. Remove the steamer basket from the pot, pour out the water, then return the squash to the pot. Add the butter, honey, and salt. Use a potato masher or immersion blender to mash the squash until smooth.

Transfer the chicken and squash to serving plates and serve right away.

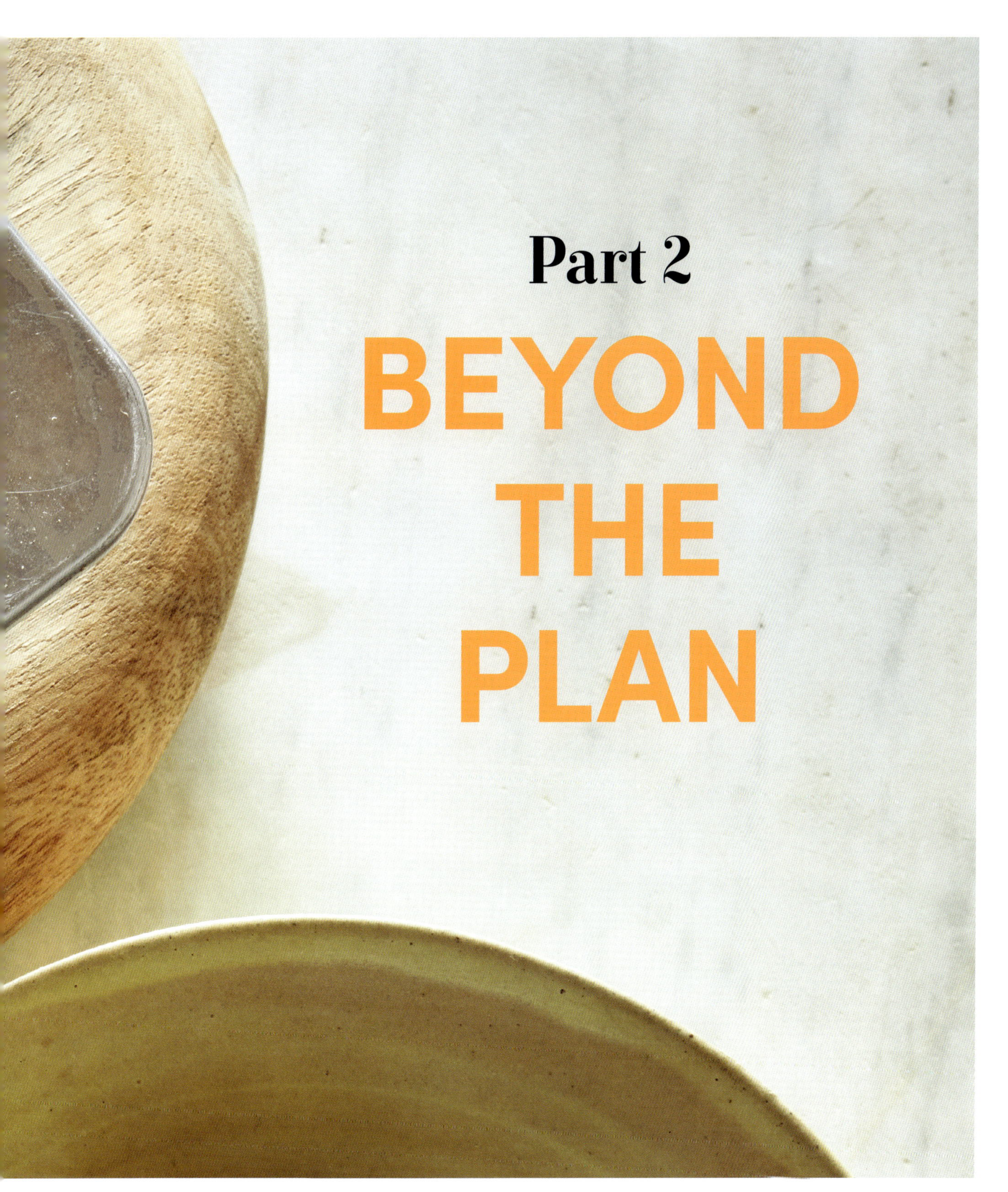

Part 2

BEYOND THE PLAN

MAKE-AHEAD BREAKFASTS

These are the recipes I rely on to get us through a week of busy mornings. My little girls are always hungry first thing, and it's a bit of a scramble to get everyone ready for school. With breakfast ready to go (straight off the counter or with a quick zap in the air fryer or microwave), we're set up for success.

As a bonus, I'm also including a recipe for our favorite smoothie. It's not exactly a make-ahead meal, but it takes minutes to make and keeps for a couple days in the fridge, so one batch lasts us for another morning or two!

PREP TIME: 10 minutes

COOK TIME: 10 minutes per batch

Fun Morning Pancakes

Pancakes make for "fun mornings" in our house—all it takes is throwing a few sprinkles or mini chocolate chips into the batter to delight my girls. This recipe makes just as many as we need for our family of two adults and two small children, and one or two make the perfect serving for a toddler, especially when paired with fruit, sausage, or a hard-boiled egg. This recipe is easily doubled for bigger families or bigger appetites!

Yield: 8 (5-inch) pancakes (4 servings)

1¼ cups all-purpose flour
½ cup almond flour
2 tablespoons granulated sugar
1 teaspoon baking powder
½ teaspoon baking soda
¼ teaspoon kosher salt
1 cup buttermilk or plain whole-milk yogurt (not Greek)
1 large egg
1 teaspoon vanilla extract
¼ teaspoon almond extract
1½ tablespoons rainbow sprinkles or 2 tablespoons mini chocolate chips (optional)
Avocado oil spray

TOPPING IDEAS

Butter and maple syrup
Vanilla yogurt and sprinkles
Nut butter and chocolate chips
Jam

In a large bowl, whisk together the all-purpose flour, almond flour, sugar, baking powder, baking soda, and salt. Whisk in the buttermilk, egg, vanilla, and almond extract until combined—it's fine if there are some small lumps. Stir in the sprinkles or chocolate chips, if using.

Heat a large nonstick skillet on the stove over **MEDIUM-LOW** heat. (Alternatively, you can use an electric griddle or skillet.) Lightly grease the skillet with the avocado oil spray.

Use a ¼-cup measure to portion out three or four pancakes into the pan. Cook them for 3 to 4 minutes on their first side, or until bubbles have come up all over the surface of the pancakes. Use a thin, flexible spatula to flip the pancakes. Let them cook for 2 minutes more, until they're golden brown on their second sides and cooked through. Transfer the pancakes to serving plates. Repeat with the remaining batter.

Serve with whatever toppings you like.

STORAGE INSTRUCTIONS

To store any leftover pancakes, let cool to room temperature on a wire rack, then transfer to a zip-top bag or tightly lidded container. The pancakes will keep in the refrigerator for up to 5 days or in the freezer for up to 2 months.

To reheat, microwave refrigerated pancakes for about 15 seconds or frozen ones for about 25 seconds. Alternatively, air-fry refrigerated pancakes at 350°F for 2 minutes or frozen pancakes for 3 minutes.

COOKING METHOD: waffle maker

PREP TIME: 10 minutes

COOK TIME: 5 minutes per batch

Greek Yogurt Waffles

Everyone in my house gets excited when the waffle iron comes out of the cabinet. My girls love waffles, and so do my husband and I. In order to make them more filling, I've bumped up the nutrition factor with lots of protein-packed ingredients, including almond flour, eggs, milk, and Greek yogurt. They're soft on the inside and crispy on the outside, just how we like them. I make them on the weekend and freeze any extras for enjoying during the week, toasted and topped with nut butter for a fast and hearty morning meal.

Yield: 8 waffles

- 1½ cups all-purpose flour
- ½ cup almond flour
- 2 tablespoons granulated sugar
- 2 teaspoons baking powder
- ½ teaspoon baking soda
- ¼ teaspoon kosher salt
- 1 cup plain whole-milk Greek yogurt
- 1 cup whole milk
- 2 large eggs
- ¼ cup avocado oil or other neutral oil
- 1 teaspoon vanilla extract
- ¼ teaspoon almond extract
- Avocado oil spray

TOPPING IDEAS

- Blueberries, raspberries, and/or sliced strawberries
- Butter and honey or agave nectar
- Nutella and sliced bananas
- Whipped cream and sprinkles
- Lemon curd and powdered sugar

Preheat the waffle iron, selecting the Classic and/or Medium browning setting if available.

In a large bowl, whisk together the all-purpose flour, almond flour, sugar, baking powder, baking soda, and salt.

Whisk in the yogurt, milk, eggs, oil, vanilla, and almond extract until combined—it's fine if there are some small lumps.

Lightly grease the preheated waffle iron with the avocado oil spray. Use a ½-cup measure to scoop the batter into each section of the waffle maker, then close and cook for about 5 minutes, or until the waffles are golden brown. Transfer the waffles to serving plates. Repeat with the remaining batter.

Serve with whatever toppings you like.

STORAGE INSTRUCTIONS

To store any leftover waffles, let cool to room temperature on a wire rack, then transfer to a zip-top bag or tightly lidded container. The waffles will keep in the refrigerator for up to 5 days or in the freezer for up to 2 months.

To reheat, microwave refrigerated waffles for about 30 seconds or frozen ones for about 1 minute. Alternatively, air-fry refrigerated waffles at 350°F for 3 minutes or frozen waffles for 5 minutes.

PREP TIME: 10 minutes

COOK TIME: 16 minutes (air fryer) or 20 minutes (oven)

Egg Bites to Go

Egg bites are a versatile breakfast staple that I almost always have on hand. They're baby- and toddler-friendly served on their own, and everyone-friendly when tucked into a breakfast sandwich (page 186). Options for flavoring your egg bites are endlessly customizable—just mix in whatever cheeses and vegetables your family enjoys.

Yield: 8 egg bites

- 4 large eggs
- ½ cup plain whole-milk Greek yogurt
- ½ cup shredded or crumbled cheese (see note)
- ½ cup chopped add-ins (optional; see note)
- Avocado oil spray

Grease 8 silicone muffin cups lightly with oil.

Preheat an air fryer to 300°F or a conventional oven to 325°F.

In a 4-cup liquid measuring cup with a pouring spout, whisk together the eggs and yogurt until smooth. Add the cheese and any add-ins and whisk to combine.

Working quickly before the egg mixture has a chance to settle, pour ¼ cup of the mixture into each of the muffin cups.

Bake the egg bites for 16 minutes in the air fryer or 20 minutes in the oven. (If using an oven or a toaster oven–style air fryer, place the muffin cups on the baking pan that comes with it.)

When the cooking program ends, remove the egg bites from the air fryer or oven. Let the egg bites cool in their muffin cups for 5 minutes (they will deflate a bit as they cool).

Pop the egg bites out of the muffin cups. Transfer the egg bites to serving dishes and serve warm.

NOTES: For the cheese, use shredded cheddar, Colby, Monterey Jack, mozzarella, or crumbled feta or goat cheese. For the add-ins, mix in diced bell peppers, thinly sliced green onions, diced ham or crumbled bacon, thawed frozen chopped spinach, riced cauliflower, or leftover roasted or steamed vegetables like broccoli or asparagus, chopped small. You can even add a tablespoon of sun-dried tomato or basil pesto. As long as the add-ins don't total more than ½ cup in volume, you're good.

Since I'm cooking for small children, I don't add extra salt to these egg bites beyond what's in the cheese or other add-ins. If you like, season yours with salt to taste.

STORAGE INSTRUCTIONS

Let the egg bites cool, then store in a lidded container in the fridge for up to 4 days or in the freezer for up to 2 months. Place sheets of wax paper between each layer of egg bites to prevent them from sticking together.

To reheat the egg bites, air-fry at 350°F for 3 minutes if refrigerated or 5 minutes if frozen. Microwave for 25 seconds if refrigerated or 45 seconds if frozen.

EGG BITE SANDWICHES are a convenient breakfast at home or on the go. Use a knife to smash your egg bite onto a toasted English muffin or onto half of a large slice of sourdough bread. Add a cooked breakfast sausage patty (or two sausage links, split in half lengthwise) on top of the egg bite. Top with the other half of the English muffin, or fold the sourdough bread in two, to make a sandwich. This also works well with a pita pocket, lavash wrap, or tortilla. Spread your bread first with butter or aioli, if you like.

PREP TIME: 3 minutes

COOK TIME: 6 minutes

Breakfast Quesadillas

Here's a simple breakfast you can either make ahead and reheat or just whip up on the spot in 10 minutes flat. Eggs and cheese are sandwiched between two crispy browned tortillas for a protein-packed vegetarian quesadilla. Sides of salsa and sour cream are essential for an ultimate eating experience, so everyone can dip their wedges of quesadilla and enjoy.

Yield: 1 quesadilla (serves 1 to 2; make as many as you need)

2 large eggs
⅛ teaspoon salt
A few grinds black pepper
Avocado oil spray
½ cup (2 ounces) shredded cheese (Mexican blend, Monterey Jack, Colby Jack, mozzarella, or cheddar), divided
2 (8- to 10-inch) flour tortillas

FOR SERVING

Salsa or hot sauce
Guacamole
Sour cream

In a bowl, whisk together the eggs, salt, and pepper.

Heat a medium nonstick skillet over medium heat. Grease the skillet lightly with avocado oil spray. Pour in the eggs, swirling them around in the pan to make an even layer. When the eggs are mostly set, after about 2 minutes, sprinkle ¼ cup of the cheese in an even layer over the eggs, top with a tortilla, then use a thin, flexible spatula to flip, so the eggs are on top.

Sprinkle the remaining ¼ cup of cheese over the eggs, then place the second tortilla on top. Let the quesadilla cook for about 2 minutes, until the bottom tortilla is golden brown, then flip and cook for about 2 minutes more, to brown the second tortilla.

Slide the quesadilla out of the pan onto a cutting board. Cut it into wedges and serve with salsa, guac, and sour cream on the side.

STORAGE INSTRUCTIONS

Let any leftovers cool to room temperature, then wrap with plastic wrap or store in a tightly lidded container. The quesadilla will keep in the refrigerator for up to 3 days or in the freezer for up to 2 months.

To reheat, air-fry a refrigerated quesadilla at 350°F for 3 minutes or a frozen one for 6 minutes. Alternatively, microwave a refrigerated quesadilla for about 45 seconds or a frozen one for about 1½ minutes.

PREP TIME: 10 minutes **COOK TIME:** 20 minutes

Savory Breakfast Muffins

Silicone muffin cups get a real workout in my house. I use them for Egg Bites (page 185), as muffin tin liners, and even as dividers in my kids' lunch boxes. Here, they're filled with muffin batter that's studded with ham, spinach, and cheese, for days when you'd rather have savory than sweet! These freeze great and reheat in the microwave in no time.

Yield: 12 muffins

- 2 cups all-purpose flour
- 2 teaspoons baking powder
- ½ teaspoon baking soda
- ½ teaspoon kosher salt
- ¼ teaspoon ground black pepper
- 1 cup milk
- 2 large eggs
- 4 tablespoons butter, melted and cooled
- 4 cups loosely packed baby spinach leaves, chopped fine
- 1 cup chopped cooked ham or turkey
- 1 cup (4 ounces) shredded cheddar, Gruyère, fontina, or other favorite melting cheese

Preheat the oven to 375°F. Line a standard muffin tin with silicone or parchment muffin liners.

In a large bowl, whisk together the flour, baking powder, baking soda, salt, and pepper until thoroughly combined. Add the milk, eggs, and butter and whisk until all the flour is absorbed—it's fine if there are some small lumps. Fold in the spinach, ham, and cheese.

Spoon the batter into the prepared muffin tin, filling the cups about two-thirds full.

Bake the muffins for 20 to 25 minutes, or until they are golden brown and a toothpick inserted in the middle of a muffin comes out clean.

Remove the muffins from the oven, let cool for about 5 minutes, then unmold them from their muffin cups, transfer to serving plates, and serve warm.

STORAGE INSTRUCTIONS

To store any leftover muffins, let cool to room temperature on a wire rack, then transfer to a zip-top bag or tightly lidded container. The muffins will keep in the refrigerator for up to 3 days or in the freezer for up to 2 months.

To reheat, microwave refrigerated muffins for about 30 seconds or frozen ones for about 50 seconds.

PREP TIME: 10 minutes

COOK TIME: 22 minutes (or 12 minutes for mini muffins)

Best Banana Muffins

My friend Amy makes the most delicious banana muffins, and now you can too. Her recipe is a simple, one-bowl affair, and you can tweak and adapt it endlessly. I usually add mini chocolate chips since that's what my girls like best.

Yield: 12 muffins (or 24 mini muffins)

3 medium ripe bananas
⅓ cup granulated sugar
⅓ cup avocado oil or applesauce
1 large egg
2 tablespoons plain whole-milk Greek yogurt or sour cream
1½ teaspoons vanilla extract
1 cup all-purpose flour (or ½ cup whole-wheat flour plus ½ cup all-purpose flour)
½ cup almond flour
¾ teaspoon baking soda
½ teaspoon kosher salt
¼ teaspoon cinnamon

OPTIONAL ADD-INS (PICK ONE)

½ cup chocolate chips (my girls' favorite)
½ cup chopped walnuts or pecans
½ cup finely grated carrot, zucchini, or apple
¼ cup hemp seeds
3 tablespoons nut butter
2 tablespoons chia seeds
Pinch ground cloves or nutmeg

Preheat the oven to 325°F. Line a standard or mini muffin tin with paper liners.

In a large bowl, use a potato masher or immersion blender to mash the bananas (it's fine if they're a bit lumpy). Stir in the sugar, oil, egg, yogurt, and vanilla.

Add the all-purpose flour, almond flour, baking soda, salt, and cinnamon and stir to combine. Fold in your choice of add-in (if using).

Portion out the batter into the muffins—about ¼ cup batter per muffin for standard muffins or 2 tablespoons for mini muffins.

Bake standard muffins for 22 to 25 minutes or mini muffins for 12 to 14 minutes, or until a toothpick inserted into the center of a muffin comes out clean.

Remove the muffins from the oven. Let them cool in the muffin tin for about 5 minutes, then transfer to a wire rack and allow to cool for at least 10 minutes before serving.

STORAGE INSTRUCTIONS

To store any leftover muffins, let cool to room temperature on a wire rack, then transfer to a zip-top bag or tightly lidded container. The muffins will keep at room temperature for up to 3 days, in the fridge for up to a week, or in the freezer for up to 2 months.

To reheat, microwave refrigerated muffins for about 25 seconds and frozen ones for about 45 seconds.

PREP TIME: 10 minutes **COOK TIME:** 40 minutes

Baked Oatmeal Squares

One of my gravest mistakes as a mother was not getting my kids used to eating regular ol' oatmeal out of a bowl when they were still forming their tastes. I'm still kicking myself for that one, but luckily, I've come up with a make-ahead oatmeal recipe that they enjoy very much: these chewy and sweet baked oatmeal squares. A whole dish keeps well in the fridge for a few days, or you can slice and freeze servings to defrost one at a time.

Yield: 9 to 12 servings (large or small squares)

- Butter or avocado oil spray, for greasing the pan
- 4½ cups rolled oats
- 2 teaspoons baking powder
- ½ teaspoon kosher salt
- 2 large eggs
- 2 cups whole milk
- ¼ cup maple syrup, honey, or agave nectar
- ¼ cup avocado oil or applesauce
- 1 teaspoon vanilla extract

FLAVOR ADD-INS (PICK ONE)

- Apple Cinnamon: 1 cup diced apples and 1 teaspoon ground cinnamon
- Blueberry Almond: 1 cup fresh or frozen blueberries and ½ cup sliced almonds
- Banana Nut: 2 mashed ripe bananas and ½ cup chopped walnuts or pecans

Preheat the oven to 350°F. Lightly grease a 9 x 13-inch baking dish with butter or avocado oil spray.

In a large bowl, stir together the oats, baking powder, and salt. Add the eggs, milk, maple syrup, oil, and vanilla, along with your choice of flavor add-ins. Stir until well combined.

Pour the mixture into the greased baking dish and spread it out in an even layer. Bake for 40 minutes, or until the edges are golden brown and a toothpick inserted into the center of the oatmeal comes out clean.

Remove the baked oatmeal from the oven. Let cool for at least 10 minutes, then slice into squares and serve.

STORAGE INSTRUCTIONS

Let cool to room temperature. To refrigerate, cover with plastic wrap and store in the refrigerator for up to 5 days. To freeze, wrap the squares individually in plastic wrap, then place them in a zip-top bag or tightly lidded container and freeze for up to 2 months.

To reheat, microwave refrigerated oatmeal squares for 45 seconds or frozen for 1½ minutes.

NO COOK

PREP TIME: 5 minutes, plus overnight to chill **COOK TIME:** 0 minutes

Overnight Oat Jars with Hemp and Chia

I'll admit, this one's mostly for me! I love overnight oats. The added tang from the yogurt, the eat-it-cold-from-the-fridge convenience, the boost of nutrients from hemp and chia seeds . . . one jar is enough to keep me going until lunchtime. It takes no time to put together, and the jars will keep in the fridge for 5 days. This recipe is scaled to make one serving in a pint jar—scale it up for as many servings as you need, or divide it into half-pint jars for smaller appetites.

Yield: 1 serving

½ cup rolled oats
¾ cup plain whole-milk Greek yogurt
½ cup whole milk
2 teaspoons honey or agave nectar
¼ teaspoon vanilla extract
1 tablespoon hemp seeds
1 teaspoon chia seeds
¼ teaspoon ground cinnamon
⅛ teaspoon kosher salt

OPTIONAL ADD-INS

½ cup blueberries or chopped strawberries
½ cup chopped peaches or nectarines
2 dates, pitted and chopped
1 tablespoon nut butter
⅛ teaspoon ground nutmeg, allspice, cardamom, or ginger

In a pint jar, stir together all the ingredients, along with one or two of the optional add-ins, if you like. Cover and allow to chill overnight or for up to 5 days.

Enjoy straight from the fridge.

STORAGE INSTRUCTIONS

The oats will keep in their jar, refrigerated, for up to 5 days. These don't freeze well—I like to make them on the weekend and enjoy them on weekday mornings.

PREP TIME: 10 minutes **COOK TIME:** 13 minutes

Breakfast Carrot Cake Cookies

I keep these in the freezer at all times. My girls love the novelty of having cookies for breakfast, and I don't mind giving them a cookie when it's full of nutritious ingredients like oats, almond flour, hemp seeds, and carrots. They have a soft, cakey texture, with chewy oats throughout.

Yield: 16 cookies

2½ cups rolled oats
¾ cup all-purpose flour
½ cup almond flour
¼ cup granulated sugar
1 teaspoon baking powder
1 teaspoon pumpkin pie spice (or ½ teaspoon ground cinnamon, ¼ teaspoon ground ginger, and ¼ teaspoon ground allspice)
¼ teaspoon kosher salt
½ cup whole milk
¼ cup honey
1 large egg
1 teaspoon vanilla extract
½ cup applesauce, pumpkin puree, or mashed banana
2 large carrots, peeled and grated on a fine grater or Microplane
½ cup chopped walnuts or pecans (optional)

Preheat the oven to 350°F. Line a sheet pan with parchment paper.

In a large bowl, stir together the oats, all-purpose flour, almond flour, sugar, baking powder, pumpkin pie spice, and salt. Add the milk, honey, egg, vanilla, applesauce, carrots, and walnuts (if using) and stir until well combined.

Use a 2½-tablespoon cookie scoop to portion the cookie dough onto the lined sheet pan. Wet your fingers, then lightly pat the cookies down into ½-inch-thick circles. It's fine if they're close together—these cookies do not spread much during baking.

Bake the cookies for 13 minutes, or until they are cooked through and golden brown on the bottom.

Transfer the cookies to a wire rack, let cool to room temperature, and enjoy.

STORAGE INSTRUCTIONS

Transfer leftover cookies to a tightly lidded container or zip-top bag and store in the refrigerator for up to 1 week or in the freezer for up to 2 months.

To reheat, microwave refrigerated cookies for 10 seconds or frozen cookies for 20 seconds.

VEGAN VARIATION: Substitute an equal amount of plant-based milk for the whole milk, 1 tablespoon cornstarch and 3 tablespoons water for the egg, and maple syrup or agave nectar for the honey.

PREP TIME: 15 minutes

COOK TIME: 10 minutes

French Toast Sticks

I make these when I have a loaf of bread that's about to go stale. It's a great way to transform something that would've gone to waste into a delicious breakfast. French toast sticks freeze and reheat beautifully—I make a large batch in the oven on the weekend, then reheat them in the air fryer throughout the week. Any thickly sliced bread will work well, so use whatever you have on hand.

Yield: 6 to 8 servings

- 8 thick slices Texas toast, challah, brioche, or sourdough bread
- 4 large eggs
- 1⅓ cups buttermilk
- 1 teaspoon vanilla extract
- ½ teaspoon ground cinnamon

TOPPING/DIPPING IDEAS

- Maple syrup
- Honey
- Nut butter
- Jam
- Vanilla yogurt

Preheat the oven to 400°F. Line a sheet pan with parchment paper.

Cut the slices of bread into 1½- to 2-inch-wide sticks.

In a large shallow bowl or baking dish, whisk together the eggs, buttermilk, vanilla, and cinnamon.

Dunk the sticks of bread into the egg mixture, turning them over so they're coated on both sides, then transfer them to the lined sheet pan, leaving a little space between each French toast stick so that they do not stick together.

Bake the French toast sticks for 10 minutes, until they're lightly browned and cooked through. Remove from the oven and serve right away, with whichever topping or dip you like.

STORAGE INSTRUCTIONS

After cooking, transfer the toast sticks to a wire rack to cool to room temperature, then store in a tightly lidded container or zip-top bag. The French toast sticks will keep in the refrigerator for up to 5 days or in the freezer for up to 2 months.

To reheat, air-fry the French toast sticks for 3 minutes at 400°F if refrigerated or 5 minutes if frozen.

Last-Minute Breakfasts

Occasionally, I don't have anything made ahead or ready to go for breakfast, and we're in a bit of a hurry. Those days require throwing something together fast, with minimal prep time or cleanup. Here are some of my go-tos:

COTTAGE CHEESE BOWLS: Scoop ½ cup cottage cheese into a bowl and top it with savory or sweet toppings.

On the savory side, I go for:

- Sliced Persian cucumbers and everything bagel seasoning
- Halved cherry tomatoes and za'atar
- Roasted red bell pepper strips (store-bought) and olive oil

And for sweet options:

- Frozen pineapple tidbits and agave nectar
- Chopped apples, ground cinnamon, and maple syrup
- Sliced almonds and honey

Serve savory bowls with some pita chips or crackers on the side, and sweet ones with a slice of multigrain toast or an English muffin, if you need a heartier meal.

TEXTURE TIP: If you don't like the texture of cottage cheese, just blend it up! Add the whole container to a blender or food processor, blend until smooth, then return it to the container where it'll be ready to use.

YOGURT BERRY BOWLS: Add a serving of yogurt to a bowl and top it with ½ cup or so of whatever berries you've got in your refrigerator or freezer. Add a scoop of your favorite breakfast cereal, muesli, or granola for extra energy.

TOAST WITH THE MOST: A slice of whole-grain or sourdough toast is the base, and you can go from there. Here are some of my favorite combos:

- Mashed avocado and fried egg (serve with hot sauce or ketchup)
- Almond butter and sliced banana (a sprinkle of ground cinnamon is nice)
- Ricotta cheese and honey (flaky salt optional)
- Nutella and sliced strawberries (sprinkle on sliced almonds or chopped hazelnuts for crunch)
- Lemon curd and raspberries (sprinkle on a few hemp seeds to make it more filling)
- Cream cheese and jam (sprinkle on sunflower seeds or walnut pieces)

TIP: If you're serving young kids, let them add the final topping. They're more likely to be excited about breakfast if they get to help make it!

BREAKFAST, BUT MAKE IT '90S: My elder millennial heart cannot resist a simple, zero-effort breakfast like the ones my parents used to keep around for my brother and me. Boxed cereal and milk. Buttered toast. A bagel with cream cheese. A store-bought toaster pastry or cereal bar. A frozen waffle with maple syrup. Yogurt and granola. Sometimes, you really truly do not have to try very hard! It's all about balance.

PREP TIME: 5 minutes

COOK TIME: 0 minutes

Our Favorite Smoothie

There's pretty much always a jar full of smoothie in my fridge, ready for my girls to sip for breakfast or snack time. It's an easy way to ensure they're getting a bunch of fresh fruit in their tummies, along with nutritious add-ins like hemp seeds, chia seeds, or sea moss gel.

Yield: 6 (1-cup) servings

1 large ripe banana
1 cup frozen pineapple chunks
1 cup frozen mango chunks
1 cup frozen blueberries
¼ cup hemp seeds
2 cups pineapple juice
½ cup water

Add all the ingredients to a blender in the order listed. Start the blender at **LOW** speed, then gradually increase to **HIGH** speed to ensure all of the ingredients are blending well. Blend for about 45 seconds, or until the smoothie is fully blended with no chunks of fruit remaining. If you have difficulty getting your smoothie to blend, turn off the blender, add another splash of juice or water, stir, and blend once more.

Pour the smoothie into glasses and serve.

STORAGE INSTRUCTIONS

Any leftovers will keep in a tightly lidded container in the fridge for up to 2 days.

VARIATIONS: Change up the ingredients in your smoothie however you please. As long as you keep the quantities of fruit and liquid the same, it will blend up well. Sub in cherries, raspberries, strawberries, or a berry blend for the blueberries. Use frozen peaches or nectarines in place of the pineapple or mango. Add up to 2 tablespoons sea moss gel or chia seeds if you like. If using chia seeds, soak them in the water or juice for a few minutes before adding to your smoothie.

BAKED GOODS (SAVORY AND SWEET)

These are my most basic and most repeated baked goods—classics that my family loves and that I enjoy making, too. Elaborate, time-consuming baking projects aren't my forte—these are the simple and delicious recipes that I come back to again and again, and they don't require a whole lot of effort or expertise. I also think that baking projects are often the most fun to get kids involved with—my girls love to measure, mix, stir, and play with dough.

When there isn't a whole lot of extra time to be had, I absolutely rely on store-bought versions of many of these. If you've got the time, though, it's really wonderful to enjoy homemade baked goods once in a while!

- All-Purpose Fridge Dough (Pitas, Pizza, etc.)
- Dinner Rolls, Hot Dog Buns, or Burger Buns
- Cornbread
- Buttermilk Biscuits or Scones
- Zucchini-Carrot Bread
- Chocolate Chip Toffee Cookies
- Microwave Ramekin Chocolate Cake

PREP TIME: 15 minutes (plus 40 minutes to proof)

All-Purpose Fridge Dough (Pitas, Pizza, etc.)

This is the most basic dough ever, with just four ingredients: flour, yeast, salt, and water. I make it in the stand mixer, so it takes very little work to throw together. Once it's had a chance to sit for a quick rise, it can live in the refrigerator for up to 3 days, until you're ready to use it for pitas, pizza, flatbread, garlic knots, or breadsticks.

Yield: Dough for 2 (12-inch) pizzas, 12 pitas, 4 flatbreads, 16 garlic knots, or 16 breadsticks

- 4 cups bread flour or all-purpose flour
- 2 teaspoons instant yeast
- 2 teaspoons kosher salt
- 1½ cups warm water (115°F)

Combine the flour, yeast, and salt in the bowl of a stand mixer and stir to combine. Fit the stand mixer with the hook attachment, then add the water and knead at **LOW** speed for 8 minutes.

Remove any dough from the dough hook and take the bowl off the mixer. Turn the dough onto a work surface and shape into a ball, then place the dough back in the bowl. Cover and place it in a warm spot in your kitchen (I like to use my oven, preheated for 1 minute on its **BAKE** setting and then turned off), and let the dough proof for about 40 minutes, or until about doubled in size.

Transfer the dough to a work surface. Divide it into however many pieces you need (see What to Make with Your Dough, page 204), and store any extra dough in a lidded container in the fridge for up to 3 days. Make sure the container is about twice the size of the dough, as it may expand in the fridge.

WHAT TO MAKE WITH YOUR DOUGH

PIZZA: Use half a batch of dough for a 12-inch pizza. On a floured work surface, roll the dough out into a 12-inch round, then top with your sauce, cheese, and toppings of choice. Bake in an air fryer (directly in the air fryer basket or on the baking sheet of an air fryer oven, lined with parchment paper or aluminum foil) at 400°F for 12 minutes or in a conventional oven (on a parchment-lined sheet pan) at 425°F (on the convection setting if it has one) for 15 minutes.

PITAS: Use half a batch of dough for 6 pitas. On a floured work surface, divide the dough into 6 pieces. Roll each one out into a 6-inch circle. Bake 2 at a time in an air fryer (directly in the air fryer basket or on the baking sheet of an air fryer oven, lined with parchment paper or aluminum foil) at 400°F for 4 minutes.

FLATBREAD: Use half a batch of dough for 2 flatbreads. Roll each piece out into a 10 x 5-inch rectangle, then top with whatever you like (I love a drizzle of olive oil, some chopped fresh rosemary, and flaky salt), then bake in an air fryer (directly in the air fryer basket or on the baking sheet of an air fryer oven, lined with parchment paper or aluminum foil) at 400°F for 12 minutes or in a conventional oven (on a parchment-lined sheet pan) at 425°F (on the convection setting if it has one) for 15 minutes.

GARLIC KNOTS: Use half a batch of dough for 8 garlic knots. Divide the dough into 8 pieces and roll them out into 6-inch-long, 1-inch-thick logs. Tie each piece of dough into a knot, then bake in an air fryer (directly in the air fryer basket or on the baking sheet of an air fryer oven, lined with parchment paper or aluminum foil) at 400°F for 12 minutes or in a conventional oven (on a parchment-lined sheet pan) at 425°F (on the convection setting if it has one) for 15 minutes. When they're just out of the oven, brush the garlic knots with a mixture of olive oil, minced garlic, and chopped fresh flat-leaf parsley. Sprinkle with grated parmesan cheese and serve warm.

BASIC BREADSTICKS: Use half a batch of dough for 8 breadsticks. Divide the dough into 8 pieces and roll them out into 6-inch-long, 1-inch-thick logs. Brush with olive oil and sprinkle with flaky salt. Bake in an air fryer (directly in the air fryer basket or on the baking sheet of an air fryer oven, lined with parchment paper or aluminum foil) at 400°F for 12 minutes or in a conventional oven (on a parchment-lined sheet pan) at 425°F (on the convection setting if it has one) for 15 minutes. Serve with a shallow bowl of olive oil and balsamic vinegar, or any other bread dip you like.

PREP TIME: 15 minutes **COOK TIME:** 13 minutes

Dinner Rolls, Hot Dog Buns, or Burger Buns

It's easy enough to buy a package of buns or rolls at the store, and in all honesty, that's usually what I do. Every once in a while, though, I whip up a batch of homemade buns and they're so, so good. If you're going to be having hot dogs, sausages, hamburgers, or sloppy joes, these will take your meal up a notch. Likewise, a batch of homemade dinner rolls makes a nice addition to any meal lacking in a starchy side dish.

Yield: 8 hot dog buns, burger buns, or dinner rolls

- 2½ cups all-purpose flour
- 1½ tablespoons granulated sugar
- 1 teaspoon active dry yeast
- 1 teaspoon kosher salt
- ½ cup plus 1 tablespoon warm water (115°F)
- 1 large egg, at room temperature
- 1½ tablespoons avocado oil or other neutral oil
- 2 tablespoons milk
- 1 tablespoon sesame seeds (optional)

Combine the flour, sugar, yeast, and salt in the bowl of a stand mixer and stir to combine. Fit the stand mixer with the hook attachment, then add the water, egg, and oil. Knead at **LOW** speed for 7 minutes.

Remove any dough from the dough hook and take the bowl off the mixer. Turn the dough out onto a work surface and shape into a ball, then place it back in the bowl. Cover and place it in a warm spot in your kitchen (I like to use my oven, preheated for 1 minute and then turned off), and let the dough proof for about 90 minutes, or until about doubled in size.

Line a sheet pan with parchment paper. Transfer the dough to a work surface. Divide it into 8 pieces, then shape it into logs for hot dog buns, or into balls for burger buns or dinner rolls. Transfer the buns or rolls to the lined sheet and let proof for another hour or so, until about doubled in size.

Preheat a traditional oven to 375°F (on the convection setting if it has one) or an air fryer to 350°F.

Brush the buns or rolls with the milk, then sprinkle with sesame seeds,

if using. Bake in a traditional oven for 13 minutes or in an air fryer for 9 minutes.

Transfer the buns or rolls to a cooling rack. Let cool to room temperature, then enjoy right away or store in a lidded container at room temperature for up to 3 days.

PREP TIME: 10 minutes (plus 15 minutes to cool)

COOK TIME: 30 minutes

Cornbread

Best when fresh out of the oven, warm cornbread truly cannot be beat for a dinnertime side dish. I make it when I'm making chili for the Super Bowl or a pork roast for company, or to go with my husband's barbecue ribs or brisket. It's on the sweeter side, with both sugar and honey included in the batter—all it needs is a little bit of butter spread on top.

Yield: Serves 6

Avocado oil spray
1 cup all-purpose flour, plus more for the pan
1 cup cornmeal
¼ cup granulated sugar
1 teaspoon baking powder
½ teaspoon baking soda
½ teaspoon kosher salt
1 cup buttermilk
½ cup (1 stick) butter, melted and cooled, plus room-temperature butter for serving
2 large eggs
¼ cup honey or agave nectar

Preheat the oven to 375°F. Grease an 8-inch square baking pan with avocado oil spray and dust with flour.

In a large bowl, stir together the flour, cornmeal, sugar, baking powder, baking soda, and salt. Add the buttermilk, butter, eggs, and honey and stir until well combined.

Transfer the batter to the prepared baking pan and spread it out in an even layer. Bake for 30 minutes, or until a toothpick in the center comes out clean.

Let cool for about 15 minutes, then slice and serve warm, with butter for spreading on top.

NOTE: Alternatively, you can bake the cornbread in an air fryer oven, with the baking pan on top of the air fryer's baking sheet. Bake at 325°F for 30 minutes.

PREP TIME: 10 minutes **COOK TIME:** 12 minutes

Buttermilk Biscuits or Scones

I love baking with buttermilk. It makes everything it touches tender and tangy, from pancakes to cornbread to these drop biscuits or scones. If you want biscuits, leave the dough as is. For scones, mix in fruit or chocolate chips. Whichever way you go, they'll be delicious.

Yield: 8 biscuits or scones

- 2 cups all-purpose flour
- 2 teaspoons baking powder
- 1 teaspoon kosher salt
- ½ teaspoon baking soda
- ½ cup (1 stick) butter, frozen
- 1 cup buttermilk
- 1 cup chopped fresh fruit (apples, strawberries, peaches, or pears) or ½ cup raisins or chocolate chips (optional)

Preheat a traditional oven to 425°F (on the convection setting if it has one) or an air fryer to 400°F. Line a sheet pan (or the baking sheet of an air fryer oven) with parchment paper.

In a large bowl, stir together the flour, baking powder, salt, and baking soda. Use a coarse grater to grate the butter into the bowl with the dry ingredients, working quickly so that it doesn't melt in your hand. Stir in the butter, making sure all of the pieces are coated with flour and there aren't any big clumps of butter.

Add the buttermilk, then stir just until the dry ingredients are absorbed. If making scones, fold in the fruit or chocolate chips.

Use a ⅓-cup measure to portion the dough out directly onto the lined sheet. Bake in a traditional oven for 12 minutes or in an air fryer for 10 minutes.

To store any leftover biscuits or scones, let cool to room temperature on a wire rack, then transfer to a zip-top bag or tightly lidded container. They will keep in the refrigerator for up to 5 days or in the freezer for up to 2 months.

To reheat, microwave refrigerated biscuits or scones for about 25 seconds or frozen ones for about 50 seconds. Alternatively, air-fry refrigerated biscuits or scones at 350°F for 5 minutes or frozen ones for 8 minutes.

PREP TIME: 10 minutes (plus 1 hour to cool)

COOK TIME: 1 hour

Zucchini-Carrot Bread

I almost always have a sweet baked good on the counter for my family to enjoy throughout the week, and much of the time, it's a loaf of this zucchini-carrot bread. It's just sweet enough, and it makes a great vehicle for a schmear of whipped cream cheese if you're so inclined. Have a slice for breakfast, a snack, or really anytime.

Yield: 1 loaf

- Avocado oil spray
- 1½ cups all-purpose flour, plus more for the pan
- 2 teaspoons pumpkin pie spice (or ½ teaspoon ground cinnamon, ¼ teaspoon ground ginger, and ¼ teaspoon ground allspice)
- ½ teaspoon baking soda
- ½ teaspoon kosher salt
- 2 large eggs
- ¼ cup milk
- ½ cup avocado oil or other neutral oil
- ⅔ cup granulated sugar
- ⅔ cup old-fashioned rolled oats
- 1 (8-ounce) zucchini, grated
- 2 large carrots, peeled and grated

Preheat the oven to 325°F (on the convection setting if it has one). Grease a large 9 x 5-inch loaf pan with avocado oil spray and dust with flour.

In a large bowl, stir together the flour, pumpkin pie spice, baking soda, and salt. Add the eggs, milk, oil, and sugar and stir to combine. Using a spoon or spatula, gently fold in the oats, zucchini, and carrots. Do not overmix the batter.

Transfer the batter to the prepared loaf pan. Bake the loaf for 1 hour, or until a toothpick inserted in the middle of the loaf comes out clean (or with a few dry crumbs attached). (Alternatively, you can use an instant-read thermometer to check the temperature of the loaf—it should be 190°F or higher.)

Remove the bread from the oven and let cool to room temperature in the pan before slicing.

NOTE: You can also bake this loaf in an air fryer at 300°F (directly in the air fryer basket or on the baking sheet of an air fryer oven, lined with parchment paper or aluminum foil). Begin checking for doneness at the 50-minute mark.

PREP TIME: 15 minutes **COOK TIME:** 12 minutes

Chocolate Chip Toffee Cookies

These cookies are a 10 out of 10, according to all my friends and family who've enjoyed them. I always keep a bag of frozen cookie dough balls on hand so I'm ready to pop a few into the oven at a moment's notice. They're the best surprise dessert there is, especially when paired with a glass of cold milk or a mug of coffee. I've also been known to sub out the toffee and chocolate chips for 14 ounces chopped-up chocolate candy bars after Halloween.

Yield: about 26 cookies

- 1 cup (2 sticks) butter, at room temperature
- 1 cup granulated sugar
- 1 cup dark brown sugar
- 1½ teaspoons kosher salt
- 2 large eggs
- 2 teaspoons vanilla extract
- 3 cups all-purpose flour
- 1 teaspoon baking soda
- ½ teaspoon baking powder
- ½ (8-ounce) bag Heath English toffee baking bits or 1 (4-ounce) Heath bar, crushed into small pieces
- 1 (10-ounce) bag dark chocolate chips

In a stand mixer fitted with the paddle attachment, cream the butter, granulated sugar, brown sugar, and salt on **HIGH** speed for about 3 minutes, until fluffy and lightened in color, scraping down the sides of the bowl halfway through. Add the eggs and vanilla and beat on medium speed for about 30 seconds, just until combined.

Scrape down the sides of the bowl, then add the flour, baking soda, and baking powder. Mix on **LOW** for about 20 seconds, until the flour is mostly incorporated.

Scrape down the sides of the bowl once more. Add the toffee bits and chocolate chips, then mix on **LOW** for 15 seconds, just until they're evenly mixed into the dough.

Line a sheet pan with parchment paper or plastic wrap. Use a 2½-tablespoon scoop to portion out scoops of cookie dough onto the sheet—it's fine if they're touching. Freeze for at least 2 hours, then transfer to a freezer-safe container or zip-top bag and store in the freezer for up to 3 months.

When ready to bake, preheat the oven to 350°F or air fryer to 325°F. Line a sheet pan with parchment paper or aluminum foil. Place a few (or more than a few!) frozen portions on the lined sheet, about 2 inches apart, and bake for 12 to 15 minutes. (Alternatively, bake in an air fryer at 325°F for 11 minutes.)

Remove the cookies from the oven and firmly bang the sheet on the counter a few times to make the cookies flatter and cracklier in texture. Let them cool for 5 minutes, then transfer to a wire rack to cool to room temperature—or enjoy them warm!

NOTE: Of course, you can also bake the cookies right after you mix up the dough, without freezing. Just reduce the cooking time by 2 minutes.

COOKING METHOD: microwave (ramekin)

PREP TIME: 5 minutes (plus 10 minutes to cool)

COOK TIME: 1 minute

Microwave Ramekin Chocolate Cake

Whether you need a last-minute birthday treat or a dessert to enjoy after the kids are asleep, this is such a good one. It's a dark, rich chocolate cake with melty chocolate chips, and it just happens to be egg-free (and dairy-free if you use plant-based milk). I like to use an 8-ounce ramekin for pretty presentation if I'm making one of these for a special occasion, but it also works great in any coffee mug you've got.

Yield: 1 single-serving cake

- 2 tablespoons all-purpose flour
- 2 tablespoons granulated sugar
- 2 tablespoons Dutch-process cocoa powder
- ¼ teaspoon baking powder
- Pinch kosher salt
- 3 tablespoons milk
- 1 tablespoon avocado oil or other neutral oil
- ½ teaspoon vanilla extract
- 1½ tablespoons chocolate chips

Add the flour, sugar, cocoa powder, baking powder, salt, milk, oil, and vanilla to an 8-ounce ramekin or a coffee mug. Use a mini silicone spatula or coffee spoon to stir everything together until evenly combined. Sprinkle the chocolate chips on top.

Microwave the cake for 1 minute. Let it cool in the ramekin for 10 minutes, then enjoy.

NOTE: For an even more decadent dessert, top the cake with a little powdered sugar, a dollop of whipped cream, or a scoop of ice cream and some chocolate syrup just before serving.

Ball
MOUTH

WHAT'S FOR LUNCH?

Many meal prep plans only address dinners, which makes sense—many of us eat lunches on the run or at work and don't really think of lunch as a family affair, with everyone eating the same thing. My husband and I both work from home most days, whereas our kids are at their respective schools, one of which provides food and one doesn't. So the weekday lunch game usually plays out with me cobbling together leftovers from the night before, my husband making himself a quick hot dog or burger (paired with a soup or leftover side dish if there's some in the fridge), my oldest getting a packed lunch (which is really a box of various snacks to tide her over until she gets home in the early afternoon), and my youngest enjoying whatever they feed her at her preschool.

When lunchtime rolls around and I need to throw something together from the fridge, I want it to be fast and easy. All of these meals come together in 15 minutes or less, making them ideal for a no-fuss midday meal.

Leftovers Makeovers

My favorite way to make a lunch is to repurpose dinner food into a salad, sandwich, flatbread, or wrap. Here are some simple templates for you to reference, then use with whatever's on hand:

SALAD: Add a layer of chopped romaine, baby spinach, or spring mix to a large bowl. Add some leftover cooked protein on top of the lettuce, along with any leftover cooked vegetables if you have them. Top with leftover vinaigrette or sauce—such as Honey-Mustard Sauce (page 15), Salsa Verde (page 14), or really almost any no-cook sauce—or store-bought dressing, or just some oil, vinegar, salt, and pepper if you don't have any sauce or dressing on hand. Optional tasty add-ins include sliced avocado, crumbled or grated cheese, and/or something crunchy (broken-up chips or crackers, store-bought croutons or fried onions/shallots, or roasted and salted nuts or seeds are my go-tos). And if you don't have any leftover protein, some canned chickpeas or black beans are an easy option.

SANDWICH: We almost always have some kind of sandwich-friendly bread on hand. Whether it's sliced sourdough, ciabatta or hoagie rolls, or a store-bought loaf of seeded whole-grain or sprouted bread, there's something that can be made into a handheld lunch. I go for a sandwich when there's a good amount of leftover meat to use up, such as some pork tenderloin, roasted chicken, or even a few meatballs that can be sliced up. First, I spread some sort of condiment onto the bread, whether it's store-bought mayo and mustard or a condiment I've made that week, such as Paprika Aioli (page 82). Next, on goes the leftover protein, followed by some salad greens and, if we have them in the house, slices of tomato and onion. You can also tuck a slice of cheese in there if you have some.

FLATBREAD: This is such a fancy-looking lunch, but it's so easy to make. If you have pita, naan, or other flatbread that needs using up, just spread on a sauce—try leftover Broccoli Pesto (page 32), Salsa Verde (page 14), or Chimichurri (page 48). Chop up leftover protein and vegetables and sprinkle them on top of the sauce, then top everything off with a generous sprinkle of your favorite shredded cheese. Into the air fryer for about 5 minutes at 400°F and you've got a crisped-up, piping-hot flatbread to enjoy.

WRAP: You can use up just about any leftovers by eating them in the form of a wrap. Just pile whatever you've got into a warmed tortilla, fold it like a burrito, and enjoy it with some leftover sauce or vinaigrette on the side for dipping or spooning onto each bite as you go. Oregano-spiked Chicken Meatballs and Spinach Orzo wrapped in a tortilla with Tzatziki (page 47) on the side, Steak Bites and Quinoa Salad in a wrap with Chimichurri (page 48) for dipping, leftover Shrimp and Black Bean and Corn Salad in a wrap with Lime Crema (page 133) . . . so many meals lend themselves well to wrap-ification.

No-Leftovers Sandwiches

As I mentioned earlier, my husband usually makes himself a hot dog or a burger for lunch. We always keep a package of hot dogs in the fridge and some buns, along with a variety of burger patties in the freezer, ready to pop into the air fryer as needed. Trader Joe's has a lot of good frozen patties, including shrimp, salmon, buffalo, turkey, and veggie varieties. And tomatoes, onions, iceberg lettuce, and pickles are staples on our grocery list, so there's never an excuse to get takeout. A handful of tater tots or fries on the side is a welcome addition, too, and we usually keep a bag or two of those in the freezer.

And then, of course, there are your basic, no-frills sandwiches, like peanut butter and jelly (or jam, honey, or banana), ham or turkey and cheese, tuna or egg salad . . . I don't have to give you instructions for those, though!

Mostly Pantry Soup

I have a go-to vegetable and bean soup that takes very little effort and comes together in about 25 minutes. That's a little longer than I like for a lunch recipe, but at least with a pressure cooker that time is nearly all hands-off. Into the pot go a glug of olive oil, a cup of store-bought mirepoix, a quart of chicken or vegetable broth, a bag of frozen mixed vegetables, a 14-ounce can of petite diced tomatoes, and a can of kidney or cannellini beans. Just 5 minutes at **HIGH** pressure and it's done. I'll throw everything in around 11:30, go get a little more work done, then come back at noon to a fully cooked soup, ready to eat with some crusty bread or cheesy toast on the side.

Baby and Toddler Snack Packs

When I pack up my preschooler's lunchbox, there's such a variety of options that it's more of a snack box. The bento-style containers she brings to school have four or five sections, which provide an easy template to follow each day. I always include:

- a fresh fruit or vegetable (or both)
- something with protein (usually some cubed cheese or a few slices of turkey pepperoni)
- crackers
- dried fruit, fruit leather, fruit snacks, or a fruit pouch
- a healthy-ish bar, muffin, or other treat

At this point it's a no-brainer process for me to fill up all the sections of her lunchbox to make for a balanced, snacky meal.

LAZY AND LAST-MINUTE MEALS

Yes, I know this is a meal prep–focused book, but sometimes I just don't have the hours or the energy to prep in advance. My family makes it through those weeks with meals that are put together with a few store-bought components, easy to pull from the freezer (if I've planned that far) or grab at the grocery store just before dinnertime. Most large grocery stores have a good variety of prepared foods and sauces, and it just takes a little creativity to turn them into a balanced meal. My favorite place to shop for these lazy meal components is Trader Joe's—their prepared frozen foods section really can't be beat for quality and variety at a reasonable price.

What follows is a selection of my family's favorite lazy dinners, which hopefully will inspire you on nights when it's tempting to order takeout (which often costs much more than even prepared grocery store items). A short grocery list and a short cooking time make all of these dinners easy to pull off, no matter your schedule.

Protein + Simple Sides

BREADED CHICKEN FILLETS, CHEESE, MARINARA, FROZEN VEGETABLES: Air-fry the frozen breaded chicken fillets according to the package instructions, adding a slice of provolone on top of each fillet during the last 2 minutes of cooking. Meanwhile, cook the frozen mixed vegetables according to the package instructions. Serve the chicken with marinara ladled on top, and the vegetables on the side.

FISH NUGGETS OR STICKS, PINTO BEANS, TORTILLAS, COLESLAW: Air-fry the fish nuggets or sticks according to the package instructions. Drain and rinse the canned beans, and warm in the microwave for 1½ minutes, stirring halfway through heating. Serve in warmed fajita-size flour tortillas, topped with coleslaw (store-bought or from a kit), with the warmed beans on the side.

FROZEN PEPPERS AND ONIONS, SAUSAGES, HOAGIE ROLLS, MOZZARELLA CHEESE: Air-fry a 1-pound bag of frozen fire-roasted peppers and onions at 400°F for 8 minutes. Add 12 ounces sliced, fully cooked sausages, shake to combine, and air-fry for another 5 minutes. Spoon the mixture into rolls, sprinkle cheese on top, and air-fry for another 2 minutes.

VEGETABLE AND NOODLE STIR (AIR) FRY: Air-fry a 1-pound bag of frozen stir-fry vegetables at 400°F for 8 minutes. Add 8 ounces no-boil noodles and ¼ cup stir-fry sauce, toss with tongs to combine, and air-fry for another 4 minutes.

BULGOGI BEEF OR TERIYAKI CHICKEN, RICE, QUICK CUCUMBER SALAD: Cook a package of frozen bulgogi beef or teriyaki chicken according to the package's skillet instructions. Microwave a package of frozen cooked rice according to the package instructions. Transfer the meat and rice to serving bowls. Slice up 1 Persian cucumber per serving. Add the cucumbers to the side of each bowl, then sprinkle them with rice vinegar, toasted sesame oil, and sesame seeds.

PESTO SHRIMP, CHERRY TOMATOES, CRUSTY BREAD: Thaw a 1-pound package of shrimp according to the package instructions. Cook the shrimp in a large skillet with 1 tablespoon olive oil. When the shrimp are cooked through, turn off the heat and stir in ½ cup pesto. Transfer to serving plates, sprinkle some halved cherry tomatoes on top, and serve with crusty bread alongside.

PIZZA, SALAD: Prepare your favorite frozen pizza according to the package instructions. Toss your favorite Italian-style or Caesar salad kit. Transfer the pizza and salad to plates and serve.

Sandwiches and Wraps

VEGGIE BURGER MELTS: Cook veggie patties in the air fryer according to the package instructions. In the last 2 minutes of cooking, add a slice of cheddar on top of each patty. Sandwich the patties between slices of buttered rye or whole-wheat bread, air-fry for another 4 minutes, and serve.

CHICKEN AND SALAD PITA POCKETS: Stuff warmed pitas with grilled chicken strips and the Mediterranean-style salad kit of your choice.

CHICKEN CAESAR FLATBREADS: Air-fry some breaded chicken tenders. Sprinkle shredded Italian cheese blend onto flatbreads or pizza crust and air-fry or bake in the oven for a few minutes, until the flatbreads are warmed and the cheese is melting. Toss chopped romaine lettuce with Caesar dressing, then pile it on top of the flatbreads. Chop up the chicken tenders and scatter them on top.

SAUSAGE AND COLESLAW WRAPS: Air-fry sliced kielbasa or other smoked pork sausages for 5 minutes at 400°F. Add to a warmed tortilla, along with some coleslaw (premade or a kit).

RANCH CHICKEN WRAPS: Toss chopped romaine lettuce with ranch dressing. Add to a warmed tortilla, along with shredded rotisserie chicken.

KABOB WRAPS: Prepare a package of frozen naan according to the package instructions (or warm up naan from the bread section of the grocery store). Prepare a package of kabobs according to the package instructions. Place 2 kabobs on each naan, add a dollop of Greek yogurt or tzatziki, then top with some sliced Persian cucumbers and cherry tomatoes.

ASIAN-INSPIRED SALAD AND SHRIMP WRAPS: Toss an Asian-style salad kit. Dampen a sheet of rice paper, then roll it up with ½ cup of the salad and a few cooked shrimp (thawed from frozen). Repeat until you run out of ingredients. Serve the rolls with peanut sauce or sesame dressing.

One-Pot/-Pan Meals

PESTO GNOCCHI WITH MEATBALLS AND PEAS: Prepare frozen gnocchi and meatballs according to the package instructions. Toss with pesto and thawed frozen peas.

CHICKEN CHILI VERDE WITH RICE: Add 1½ pounds boneless, skinless chicken breasts, cut into 2-inch pieces, to a pressure cooker, along with a 12-ounce jar of salsa verde. Add a raised wire rack on top of the chicken and place a 1½-quart stainless-steel bowl on the rack. Add 1½ cups long-grain white rice and 1½ cups chicken or vegetable broth to the bowl. Pressure-cook at high pressure for 12 minutes, with a **QUICK** pressure release. Fluff up the rice, shred the chicken, transfer to bowls, and serve with sour cream and shredded Mexican cheese blend at the table.

ORZO AND SAUSAGE SKILLET: Slice 12 ounces of fully cooked sausages into ½-inch-thick rounds. Sauté them in a large skillet with 1 tablespoon olive oil. Add 1½ cups orzo pasta, a 14-ounce can of petite diced tomatoes, a 12-ounce bag of frozen mixed vegetables, and 3 cups chicken or vegetable broth. Bring to a simmer, then turn down to medium-low and simmer for about 12 minutes, stirring occasionally, until the pasta is cooked through and most of the liquid is absorbed. Serve with grated parmesan cheese.

PLUSSED-UP STORE-BOUGHT FRIED RICE: Prepare a package of frozen fried rice according to the package instructions. During the last 2 minutes of cooking, toss in 2 cups diced rotisserie chicken or baked tofu, sliced green onions, and a little soy sauce.

TACO SKILLET: In a large skillet, sauté 1 pound 90% lean ground beef over medium heat. Add a packet of taco seasoning, a 15-ounce can of corn (drained), a 15-ounce can of beans (drained and rinsed), and a package of thawed frozen rice. Cook until warmed through, transfer to serving bowls, and serve with sour cream and shredded Mexican cheese blend.

KOREAN-INSPIRED GROUND CHICKEN SKILLET: In a large skillet, sauté 1 pound 96% lean ground chicken over medium heat until cooked through and crumbly. Add 1½ cups frozen mixed vegetables and sauté until warmed through. Add 2 tablespoons soy sauce, 2 tablespoons gochujang, and 1 teaspoon garlic powder and toss to combine. Turn off the heat, then stir in 2 teaspoons toasted sesame oil and a package of thawed frozen rice. Transfer to bowls and serve, topped with sliced green onions, if you have some on hand.

CURRY NOODLES AND TOFU: In a large skillet, heat 2 tablespoons avocado oil over medium heat. Add 1 package extra-firm or super-firm tofu, sliced into 1-inch pieces, and sauté until golden brown. Add 1 package no-boil noodles and sauté for about 5 minutes, until they are cooked through. Add 1 (16-ounce) jar of Thai curry simmer sauce, stir to combine, and let simmer for a few minutes. Transfer to bowls and serve with chopped fresh cilantro on top, if you have some on hand.

Quick and Easy Bowls

BURGER SALADS: Air-fry or pan-fry 4 burger patties. Add some iceberg salad mix, halved cherry tomatoes, pickle chips, and shredded cheddar cheese to serving bowls. Chop up the patties and sprinkle them over the salads, along with drizzles of ketchup, mustard, and burger sauce.

PATTIES PARMESAN OVER PASTA: Cook a package of spaghetti according to the package instructions and toss with your favorite marinara sauce. Air-fry turkey patties or veggie patties according to the package instructions, adding a handful of Italian cheese blend on top of each patty during the last 2 minutes of cooking. Transfer the pasta to serving bowls and place a cheesy patty on top of each serving.

CARNITAS FAJITA BOWLS: Heat a 1-pound package of carnitas in a large skillet over medium heat. When the pork begins to brown and crisp up, add a 1-pound bag of fire-roasted frozen peppers and onions and sauté until warmed through. Heat up a package of frozen rice. Transfer the rice and pork-peppers mixture to serving bowls. Serve with lime wedges on the side.

CAESAR PASTA SALAD: Prepare a Caesar salad kit according to the package instructions. Prepare 8 ounces of penne pasta according to the package instructions, then rinse it under cold water to cool to room temperature. Toss the pasta with the salad, transfer to bowls, and serve. (If you like, you can also add some diced or shredded rotisserie chicken.)

TORTELLINI AND SAUSAGE BOWL: Cook a 9-ounce package of tortellini according to the package instructions. Air-fry 12 ounces fully cooked chicken sausages, sliced into ½-inch-thick rounds, at 375°F for 5 minutes. Transfer the tortellini and sausage to bowls and serve with warm marinara ladled on top. (You can also add a bag of frozen broccoli or mixed vegetables, thawed according to the package instructions.)

LEMONY CHICKEN AND ORZO: Prepare a package of orzo according to the package instructions. Shred the breast meat of a rotisserie chicken, toss it with the juice of 1 lemon, 2 tablespoons olive oil, and ½ teaspoon dried oregano, then warm through in a large skillet. Transfer the orzo and chicken to bowls and serve with tzatziki on the side. (Pair with a Mediterranean salad kit if you like.)

GYOZA AND PEAS IN BROTH: In a large skillet, cook a 1-pound package of frozen gyoza according to the package directions. Warm up a quart of broth (Trader Joe's Miso Ginger Broth is my favorite for this meal, but if you can't find it, regular chicken broth or vegetable broth works well). Add 1½ cups frozen peas to the broth and let them warm through. Add the gyoza to serving bowls, then ladle the broth and peas on top.

Acknowledgments

Yet again, I've written a cookbook! And yet again, I could not have done it without the professional and personal support of so many people.

To my editor, Deb, and her assistant, Jacqueline, thank you so much for your patience as I worked on this manuscript. As anyone with a young family knows, the challenges of balancing work and domestic responsibilities are many, even when there's a lot of overlap (thankfully they do eat most of my cooking).

To my agent, Alison, you are the best. The absolute best. I cannot stress how necessary your help and guidance have been as I've continued to navigate this career of writing and cooking for a living. You know how much I love to do creative work, and I feel so lucky to have you in my corner.

To my Portland mommas, it is such a joy to continue our friendships and watch all of our sweet kiddos grow up. From the women I first met in prenatal yoga to the friends made through daycare and preschool, I am proud to know so many amazing ladies. Thank you for testing my recipes and for the ladies' nights and play dates that make life here so fun and fulfilling.

To my husband, Brendan, wow, we've sure got a full life these days, and it's only through teamwork with you, my partner in all things, that any of it is possible. Thank you for raising two adorable little people with me and sharing responsibilities so that we can both reach for our dreams.

And to my girls, Eve and Sylvie, you mean the world to me. You're the best taste testers I could ask for, and your enthusiasm around food is a big part of what makes all this hard work so worth it. The biggest part, really. Lots of love.

UNIVERSAL CONVERSION CHART

Oven temperature equivalents

250°F = 121°C
275°F = 135°C
300°F = 149°C
325°F = 162°C
350°F = 177°C
375°F = 190°C
400°F = 205°C
425°F = 218°C
450°F = 232°C
475°F = 246°C
500°F = 260°C

Measurement equivalents

Measurements should always be level unless directed otherwise.

⅛ teaspoon = 0.5 mL
¼ teaspoon = 1 mL
½ teaspoon = 2 mL
1 teaspoon = 5 mL
1 tablespoon = 3 teaspoons = ½ fluid ounce = 15 mL
2 tablespoons = ⅛ cup = 1 fluid ounce = 30 mL
4 tablespoons = ¼ cup = 2 fluid ounces = 60 mL
5⅓ tablespoons = ⅓ cup = 3 fluid ounces = 80 mL
8 tablespoons = ½ cup = 4 fluid ounces = 120 mL
10⅔ tablespoons = ⅔ cup = 5 fluid ounces = 160 mL
12 tablespoons = ¾ cup = 6 fluid ounces = 180 mL
16 tablespoons = 1 cup = 8 fluid ounces = 240 mL

Time and Temperature Chart for Fresh and Frozen Foods

FOOD	SMART PROGRAM	COOKING TEMPERATURE	COOKING TIME	ACCESSORY	RACK POSITION AND NOTES
Asparagus	**AIR FRY**	400°F/205°C	4 minutes	Cooking pan	Middle position; turn partway
Beef jerky	**DEHYDRATE**	135°F/57°C	4 to 5 hours	Air frying basket on oven rack	Middle or highest position; set it and forget it
Beef steak	**AIR FRY**	400°F/205°C	13 to 15 minutes	Cooking pan	Middle position; turn partway
Cake	**BAKE**	355°F/179°C	30 minutes	Cake pan or baking dish on cooking pan	Lowest position; set it and forget it
Cauliflower florets	**AIR FRY**	350°F/177°C	10 to 15 minutes	Cooking pan	Middle position; turn partway
Corn, on the cob	**ROAST**	450°F/232°C	7 minutes	Cooking pan or air frying basket on oven rack	Middle position; turn partway
Corn dogs	**AIR FRY**	400°F/205°C	15 minutes	Air frying basket on oven rack	Middle position; turn partway
Chicken, rotisserie-style	**ROAST**	380°F/193°C	45 minutes	Rotisserie spit	Set it and forget it
Chicken, quartered	**ROAST**	400°F/205°C	18 minutes	Cooking pan	Middle position; turn partway
Chicken nuggets, frozen	**BROIL**	400°F/205°C	10 minutes	Cooking pan	Middle position; turn partway

FOOD	SMART PROGRAM	COOKING TEMPERATURE	COOKING TIME	ACCESSORY	RACK POSITION AND NOTES
Chicken wings, fresh	**AIR FRY**	400°F/205°C	10 to 12 minutes	Cooking pan or air frying basket on oven rack	Middle position; turn partway
Chicken wings, frozen	**AIR FRY**	400°F/205°C	12 minutes	Cooking pan or air frying basket on oven rack	Middle position; turn partway
Cupcakes	**BAKE**	365°F/187°C	13 to 14 minutes	Silicone muffin cups on cooking pan	Lowest position; set it and forget it
Eggs, large, in shell	**AIR FRY**	250°F/121°C	15 or 20 minutes (soft or hard boiled)	Air frying basket on oven rack	Middle position; set it and forget it
Falafel, frozen	**AIR FRY**	400°F/205°C	7 to 10 minutes	Cooking pan	Middle position; turn partway
Fish sticks, frozen	**BROIL**	400°F/205°C	10 to 12 minutes	Air frying basket on oven rack	Middle position; turn partway
Fries, fresh	**AIR FRY**	400°F/205°C	22 to 25 minutes	Air frying basket on oven rack	Middle position; shake partway
Fries, frozen	**AIR FRY**	400°F/205°C	12 to 15 minutes	Air frying basket on oven rack	Middle position; shake partway
Fruit leather	**DEHYDRATE**	135°F to 150°F/57°C to 66°C	6 to 8 hours	Cooking pan or air frying basket on oven rack	Middle or highest position; turn partway
Hash browns, frozen (patties or shredded)	**AIR FRY**	400°F/205°C	10 minutes	Air frying basket on oven rack	Middle position; turn partway

FOOD	SMART PROGRAM	COOKING TEMPERATURE	COOKING TIME	ACCESSORY	RACK POSITION AND NOTES
Hot dogs	**AIR FRY**	400°F/205°C	7 to 9 minutes	Air frying basket on oven rack	Middle position; set it and forget it
Mozzarella sticks, frozen	**AIR FRY**	360°F/185°C	6 minutes	Air frying basket on oven rack	Middle position; turn partway
Muffins	**BAKE**	350°F/177°C	15 minutes	Silicone muffin cups on cooking pan	Lowest position; set it and forget it
Nachos	**BROIL**	400°F/205°C	4 minutes	Cooking pan	Middle position
Pizza, frozen (thin crust)	**BAKE**	400°F/205°C	8 to 10 minutes	Cooking pan	Lowest position; set it and forget it
Potato or veggie tots, frozen	**AIR FRY**	400°F/205°C	8 to 10 minutes	Air frying basket on oven rack	Middle position; shake partway
Salmon, fresh	**BROIL**	400°F/205°C	8 to 10 minutes	Cooking pan	Middle or highest position; set it and forget it

FOOD	SMART PROGRAM	COOKING TEMPERATURE	COOKING TIME	ACCESSORY	RACK POSITION AND NOTES
Shrimp, fresh	**AIR FRY**	400°F/205°C	3 to 5 minutes	Cooking pan or air frying basket on oven rack	Middle position; turn partway
Shrimp, frozen	**AIR FRY**	380°F/193°C	4 to 6 minutes	Cooking pan or air frying basket on oven rack	Middle position; turn partway
Spanakopita, frozen	**BAKE**	320°F/160°C	10 minutes	Cooking pan	Middle position; turn partway
Taquitos	**AIR FRY**	400°F/205°C	10 minutes	Air frying basket on oven rack	Middle position; turn partway
Veggie burgers, frozen	**AIR FRY**	400°F/205°C	12 to 15 minutes	Air frying basket on oven rack	Middle position; turn partway
Waffles, frozen	**TOAST**	Select # of waffles	Toast Level 2	Oven rack	Middle position
White fish fillet, fresh	**BROIL**	400°F/205°C	3 to 4 minutes	Cooking pan	Middle or top position; set it and forget it

Cooking times are a recommendation only. Always use a meat thermometer to ensure the internal temperature reaches a safe minimum temperature. Refer to the USDA's Safe Minimum Internal Temperature Chart for more information, available online at https://www.fsis.usda.gov.

INDEX

Note: Page references in *italics* indicate photographs.

C

Q

R

S

T

U

V

W

Y

Z